IN OLD PHOTOGRAPHS

BRITAIN

AROUND HOYLAND
PEOPLE & PLACES

GEOFFREY HOWSE

Sutton Publishing Limited
Phoenix Mill · Thrupp · Stroud
Gloucestershire · GL5 2BU

First published 2002

Title page photograph: A pre-Second World War view of Earl Fitzwilliam's Elsecar Main Colliery. *(Edwin Hugh Stenton and Amy Stenton)*
Front endpaper: Wentworth Park and the 606 ft long East Front of Wentworth Woodhouse. *(Paul T. Langley Welch)*
Back endpaper: Market Street, Hoyland, April 2001. *(Author)*

British Library Cataloguing in Publication Data
A catalogue record for this book is available from the British Library.

ISBN 0-7509-3148-5

Typeset in 10.5/13.5 Photina.
Typesetting and origination by
Sutton Publishing Limited.
Printed and bound in England by
J.H. Haynes & Co. Ltd, Sparkford.

This book is dedicated to the memory of Arthur K. Clayton BEM (1901–2002) of Hoyland Common, Local Historian

The top of Rockley Lane, Birdwell (near the Cock Inn) and the bottom of Low Foulds (Rockley Crescent), towards the end of the nineteenth century. *(David Doughty collection)*

CONTENTS

The Wentworth Woodhouse fire engine, 1904. Manufactured by Merryweather, the fire engine – which is seen here shortly after its delivery – was kept in the Estate Building Yard. The Clerk of Works, Mr Dickie, can be seen on the fire engine wearing a bowler hat. *(Cyril Slinn)*

Thomas Wentworth (died 1587) and his wife Margaret (died 1592), the grandparents of Thomas Wentworth, 1st Earl of Strafford, with their daughter and head gardener. Thomas Wentworth is seen grafting a fruit tree. Note the family crest – the Wentworth griffin, on the head gardener's sleeve. A knot garden is also depicted, and a representation of Wentworth Woodhouse as it appeared in the middle of the sixteenth century can be seen beneath the coat of arms. *(Courtesy of Roy Young)*

INTRODUCTION

In this, my third book about Hoyland and the various hamlets and villages which surround it, I have tried to incorporate some aspects that have not been included in my previous books. A wealth of interesting visual information exists about the diverse personalities and the area around Hoyland and I am constantly being surprised by the generosity of local people. Since the publication of *Around Hoyland: A Second Selection* in December 2000, many people have very kindly come forward with offers of pictures and documents. Following requests and suggestions from people who have read my books, I have searched for and been offered photographs of areas and subjects that have not been covered before. Inevitably there is a certain amount of repetition, but on the whole I have been much encouraged by the diversity of new subjects which it has been possible to include here.

Hoyland forms part of and is surrounded by one of the most historically important areas in the whole of Yorkshire. Wentworth, Tankersley, Rockley, Worsborough, Blacker and Alderthwaite are just some of the older areas which are included in this book. More recent settlements include Elsecar, Hoyland Common, Birdwell, Platts Common, Harley and Chapeltown. There are also wonderful images of some of the families and individuals who have lived in or been responsible for the development of the area. A broad cross-section of local people is featured.

Change of some kind is always taking place. It is the natural way of things. Some changes are for the better but lately, much to the regret of a great many local residents, far too many changes seem to be for the worse. A major change which has affected the quality of life in Hoyland and many other places in South Yorkshire in recent years has been the decline of community spirit, resulting in a lack of organised events; and another has been the demise of the traditional public house, places where once such events were instigated, discussed and sometimes organised. In Hoyland, no longer do people of all ages visit town centre pubs. The trend to create one-bar pubs has alienated some sections of the community and created noisy, regrettably sometimes violent, inhospitable bars, which no longer have the friendly ambience of the traditional public house, which the area once possessed in abundance.

Elsecar goods station, Wath Road, before the Second World War. Aubrey Jones (porter) can be seen on the right. (*Edwin Hugh Stenton and Amy Stenton*)

A Coronation beacon built near Hoober Stand by the 2nd Wentworth Scouts in 1953. (*M. Joan Burgin*)

Another unwelcome change to have been forced on the population of Hoyland in recent years has been the changing of the names of some of its long-established pubs and inns. Hoyland's oldest licensed premises has twice been renamed, for example. This is sometimes at the expense of discarding names which have deep historical associations. It is a worrying trend, as it wipes out our links with the past. Continuity of building names, public houses in particular, can help to create a sense of pride in an area's history.

Our forefathers left a wonderful legacy of educational facilities in this area for future generations to benefit by, but in recent years many of these have disappeared. A drop in the birth rate has resulted in schools being demolished. A staggering waste of public money and in some cases an insult to the memory of distinguished benefactors has resulted from the demolition of infant, junior or primary schools. With a little inspired planning most of these buildings could have been converted to another use: workshops, community centres or even dwellings are just some of the possible uses that spring to mind. Now these buildings have been lost for ever. Such irresponsible acts are far too common and sadly, try as they might, Hoyland's elected representatives are almost powerless when it comes to deciding on major issues which would benefit the area they represent. Since 1974 major decisions have been made alongside councillors who represent areas far away from Hoyland. While ever the area is manacled to a body with outdated principles, and while bigotry and prejudice remain at the heart of local government, sensible, inspired and practical planning and decision making will continue to elude Hoyland's representatives despite their efforts.

The general quality of life for many people in Hoyland itself has declined in recent years. The town centre, once a bustling place both during the day and well into the late evening is no longer a desirable place to visit once the shops have pulled down their shutters. The occasional carrot has been thrown Hoyland's way, such as a new clock on the Town Hall, refurbished public conveniences in Market Street and surprise surprise, after years of being without one, last year Hoyland had a Christmas tree! This is simply not good enough. It is time that the area was taken seriously in hand, cleaned up, the streets made safe and services restored. The ludicrous and totally unnecessary one-way traffic system through High Street and King Street has exacerbated problems rather than solve them. The lack of a bus stop outside the Town Hall in High Street has resulted in fewer people being in the town centre in the evening. Fewer people and less traffic means that sinister and illegal acts are far more easily carried out than in days gone by. The proposed new health centre and bus station to be situated adjacent to Southgate, opposite the Library, will hardly improve matters.

On the positive side, Hoyland and the surrounding area is blessed with one of the finest public transport systems to be found anywhere in England, although some of the bus routes are somewhat idiosyncratic. Some routes being well covered, others more erratically so. It is a great pity that these services are taken for granted. Not only is there a good rail link to Sheffield, Barnsley, Wakefield, Huddersfield and Leeds but also regular daytime bus services which enable easy movement around the immediate locality, and a reasonable regular evening bus service too on several routes. Far too many people have taken to the motor car for non-essential local journeys when they could so easily use the bus services provided. The phrase 'use it or lose it' might easily be applied here. Inconsiderate acts by selfish individuals have resulted in the parking situation in Hoyland itself becoming a farce. Bad parking and illegal parking is prevalent. Adequate parking facilities exist in the town centre for a reasonable number of vehicles. Unfortunately an unreasonable number of people insist on driving into Hoyland, when many could walk or take a bus. However, instead of using the bus, people who should know better are causing unnecessary traffic and parking problems. Many more elderly residents may need to use their cars to do their shopping but many others do not. On market days they not only fill the car parks but cause chaos in residential streets. Many of the images in this book show the area when more sedate forms of transport were perfectly adequate for local people. Surely a little more thought and a little less selfishness would benefit everyone.

Hoyland Market continues to be a great asset to the area and several new shops and small businesses that have recently opened is an encouraging sign. With a little luck we may once again see the now defunct Hoyland and District Chamber of Trade, a once influential and highly respected organisation, overseeing the interests of traders and customers alike and maintaining standards, which for many years was something Hoyland could be proud of. The once popular, and no doubt profitable, annual trade fairs are much missed.

The potential that exists both within and around the Hoyland area is not being exploited. In particular, Elsecar Heritage Centre, a site of national importance, has the potential to attract large numbers of visitors on a regular basis. Surprisingly, when one considers the raw materials that are available, and sadly for the area, a feeble attempt at creating a third-rate amenity within a wonderful complex of buildings is all that has been achieved. The centre has never realised its potential. It is neither fish nor fowl. Lack of business and rising rents have driven traders and artisans away and low attendance means that many units open on certain days only, which is unfair to the few visitors who do make their way to Elsecar on weekdays. Its failure to succeed, despite vast sums of money being spent, has created a great deal of resentment locally. One only needs to visit the Black Country Museum at Dudley in Worcestershire to see what could so easily have been achieved in Elsecar, and probably with even more successful results; as a great deal of other attractions which are also of national importance are scattered throughout the surrounding area, which only serve to complement what exists on the Elsecar site.

Local people genuinely want the Heritage Centre to succeed but progress is very slow. Greater exploitation and a full restoration of the Newcomen Beam Engine, as well as a more concerted effort on work to extend the steam railway and on the restoration of the Elsecar Branch

The Estate Building Yard, Wentworth, March 1967. The Clerk of Works, John Booth, pays a visit to see how work is progressing on a coffin for the late Maud, Dowager Countess Fitzwilliam. Left to right: John Booth, Stanley Walker, Maurice Pell and an unidentified onlooker. (*Roy Young*)

The Hoyland and District Chamber of Trade float at the 1971 Gala Parade. *(Author's collection)*

of the Dearne and Dove Canal would no doubt improve matters. The creation of an artificial drift mine on a nearby site, like that at the Black Country Museum, is just one possibility, and better hands-on attractions for young people than those which were once available in the Power House would also enhance this wonderful local facility, which has the potential to attract large numbers of tourists from far afield, which would help boost the local economy.

As with other areas in the country, once children have gone through school and sometimes university, a large proportion leave the district entirely. The industries which once provided large numbers of school leavers with employment no longer exist, and this has meant an even greater migration. It has also resulted in an underclass of young people who have fallen by the wayside and who appear to have no direction in life at all. An appalling lack of knowledge about the history of the area and a distinct lack of pride in their heritage has left a whole generation with no real sense of identity. How very sad it is to witness this lack of knowledge, lack of pride and lack of interest. For too many the grass is always greener on the other side. Statistical information produced in August 2002 shows alarming results. Over fifty-five per cent of English people would choose to emigrate if they had the chance, to the USA or Australia, in particular, although the majority would prefer Spain or Portugal if language did not present a problem. If only more local people were aware of how diverse and great the raw materials are which exist in this part of South Yorkshire to develop new industries connected to leisure, tourism, arts and crafts and IT, as well as light industries connected with metal-working, carpentry and printing; and how enormous the potential to create a truly beautiful and prosperous community; with just a little more effort this corner of South Yorkshire would be a far better place.

I have attempted to include the most up-to-date information about the various subjects included in this book. I have made every effort to research each individual photograph, in an attempt to establish exactly who or what appears in it. Sometimes I have been unsuccessful. I apologise unreservedly for any errors or omissions. The views I have expressed stem from my personal observations and I accept that the reader may disagree with my assertions.

Geoffrey Howse, October 2002

1
Hoyland

Hoyland town centre, 1960s. Hoyland's much missed police station can be seen in George
Street to the left of the town hall. *(Edwin Hugh Stenton and Amy Stenton)*

This early Edwardian view shows High Street, looking towards Post Office Buildings at the junction of Milton Road and West Street. *(Chris Sharp of Old Barnsley)*

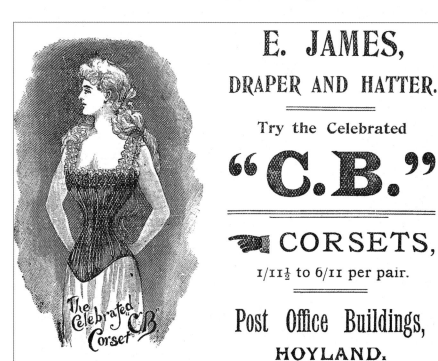

E. JAMES,

DRAPER AND HATTER.

Try the Celebrated

"C.B."

☞ CORSETS,

1/11½ to 6/11 per pair.

Post Office Buildings,

HOYLAND.

The Celebrated "C.B." Corset

This advertisement for E. James, draper and hatter, appeared in the Great Central Railway (MS&L) Sheffield to Barnsley timetable in May 1898. James's business premises can be seen above. *(Jack Oliver)*

This advertisement for Matthew's chemist also appeared in the Great Central Railway (MS&L) Sheffield to Barnsley timetable in May 1898. At that time John E. Matthew had shops in Hoyland and at 41 Church Street, Elsecar. *(Jack Oliver)*

For BACKACHE try Dr. Booth's
NOTED
GRAVEL PILLS

These Pills have been in use for the last 20 years, and for Gravel, Lumbago, Sciatica, and all pains in the back they are unequalled.

PRICE 10½d. PER BOX,

AND SOLD BY

J. E. MATTHEW,
CHEMIST,
KING ST., HOYLAND.

A group of Christians and converts in Hoyland with the Revd William Griffiths, 1920. Among the group can be seen Sarah Anne Tollerfield, who is in the back row, sixth from the left. *(David Doughty collection)*

Market Street School, 1925/6. Among those included are: Edwin Moody, Harry Joll, Maurice Wilkinson, Clifford Wilkinson, George Linley, Joyce Chambers, Cyril Fletcher, Joyce Carney, Joan Warringham, Thomas Dyson, Roland Cross and Bessie Lowbridge. *(Edwin Moody collection)*

Outside 16 Gill Street, Hoyland, in 1933: Doreen Nelder (born 1927), Margaret Nelder (born 1929) and Stanley Nelder (born 1924), children of the late Nathan Nelder and Doris his wife (née Smith). In 1930, following the death of her husband, Doris Nelder could not face living at the family home at 30 Gill Street, as she kept picturing her late husband's coffin in the front room. The family, which included Nathan Nelder's son from a previous marriage, George (1914–90 – see page 112), were offered the Manse in Hill Street, Elsecar (see page 25), but Mrs Nelder declined the offer as the graveyard was directly behind it. Instead they moved to the house seen here. *(Doreen Howse collection)*

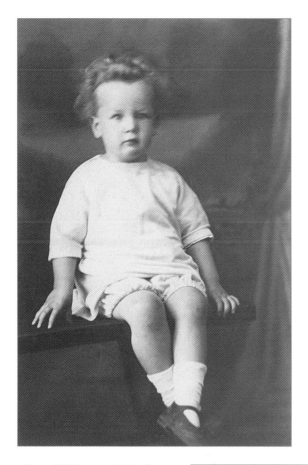

Above: William and Maud Senior's youngest child, Mary, aged four, 1927. The Seniors lived in Spring Gardens (see page 16). *(Mrs Mary Fenton)*

Above, right: Jim Bowley and Prince at 60 Longfields Crescent, 1934. *(Theresa Whittlestone)*

Right: Mrs Dunstan, -?-, Lily Bowley (née Moore), in Headlands Road, 1936. *(Theresa Whittlestone)*

Easter 1938 at 2 Croft Road, home of Roy and Anne Fletcher and their son Terry. Nellie Hull is on the left, Anne Fletcher on the right. The residents of Croft Road, along with many other places in and around Hoyland, celebrated events whenever the occasion arose. VJ Day was celebrated in 1946 by, among other festivities, the lighting of an enormous bonfire in the middle of the road. The bonfire burned for a week. When the embers had finally died down and the debris cleared, it was necessary for the council to come and fill in the enormous hole in the road's surface, which had been cracked by the intense heat. *(Theresa Whittlestone)*

No. 60 Longfields Crescent, 1939. Left to right: Roy Fletcher, Terry Fletcher, Lily Bowley, Roy's mother-in-law. Roy Fletcher appears in several photographs in this book. His wedding is featured on page 107. Roy was born in Harley. He married Anne Bowley in 1932 and worked at Wharncliffe Silkstone Colliery as a machineman collier. His wife worked at Parkin's chemists in King Street, Hoyland. Roy and Anne Fletcher lived in West Street, where their son Terry was born in 1933. There was no electricity supply in their home, so they moved to 2 Croft Road in 1936 to benefit from one (see above). Roy continued to work in the mining industry and was an ARP warden during the Second World War. He worked at Rockingham Colliery for ten years. On 8 July 1946, while working in the Silkstone seam, he suffered severe crushing injuries in an accident. He died from his injuries in the Fulwood Annexe of the Royal Infirmary, Sheffield. He was thirty-seven. *(Theresa Whittlestone)*

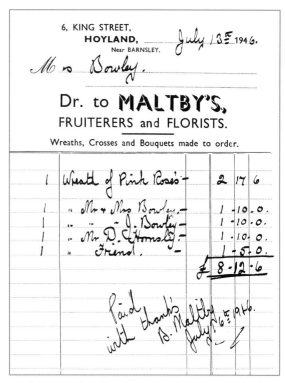

Above, left: The bill for Roy Fletcher's funeral, from Cook's, the well-known family of undertakers, established in Hoyland since 1874. Roy was buried in Kirk Balk Cemetery. *(Theresa Whittlestone) Right:* Anne Bowley's bill for flowers from Maltby's, for Roy's funeral. *(Theresa Whittlestone)*

Above, left: Longfields Crescent, 1939. Left to right: Jim Bowley jnr, Roy Fletcher, Anne Fletcher and Lily Bowley. *(Theresa Whittlestone) Right:* Jim Bowley jnr, son of Jim and Lily Bowley, was born during the First World War. He joined the Royal Artillery in 1940, shortly before Dunkirk, and not long afterwards was taken prisoner in France after he had been badly injured. He had shrapnel wounds and sustained other injuries, which included several broken bones, when he was run over by a tank. He was eventually transported to Stalag 38B, and is seen there (on the left) with his fellow POWs. *(Theresa Whittlestone)*

Dennis Cowood (originally of Warren Lane, Chapeltown) and Lillian (née Senior) his wife, with their son Gerald, c. 1942. Dennis worked for the Prudential Insurance Company but not under the direction of his father-in-law, William Senior (see below), as the latter did not want to be accused of nepotism as his son-in-law advanced within the company. The family lived in Mount Crescent, Hoyland. One day on a visit to Barnsley, after buying some sweets to give to his cousin later, Gerald, then aged fifteen, crossed the road in front of a stationary omnibus, straight into the path of a car, which knocked him over and killed him. Gerald can be seen as a pageboy on page 111 at his aunt Blanche's wedding in 1938. (*Mary Fenton*)

Mr and Mrs William Senior, of Spring Gardens. The Seniors moved to their large and comfortable home in Spring Gardens, from Warren Lane, Chapeltown. William Senior worked as District Superintendent for the Prudential Insurance Company. Maud Senior (née Pashley) had one son and four daughters by her husband: Percy, Lillian, Constance, Blanche (see page 111) and Mary (later Mrs Fenton). Blanche was a well-known figure in Hoyland, as she worked at Cross's shop in the town centre. William Senior died in 1951 aged seventy-four. Maud died in 1952, also aged seventy-four. (*Mary Fenton*)

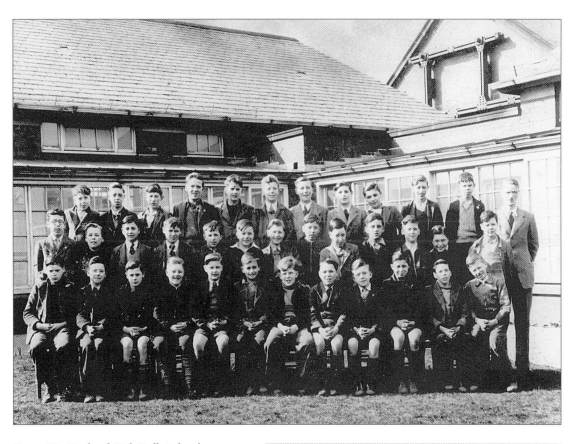

Form 2B, Hoyland Kirk Balk School,
15 March 1951. Back row, left to right:
B. Foster, -?-, ? Hodgson, ? White, I. Wroe,
? Shaw, ? Joynes, ? Dewhirst, T. Brown,
? Norris, ? Quinney. Second row: D. Doughty,
? Caswell, J. Holling, C. Wooton, ? Cooper,
K. Ackroyd, -?-, A. Blackburn, ? Drinkwater,
B. Lang, ? Fletcher, -?-, I. Brown. Front row:
? Allott, -?-, -?-, B. Moxon, K. Pickering,
? Stothart, ? Moore, A. Wooton, ? Nixon, -?-,
L. Blackburn, T. Miles. Schoolmaster:
Mr F. Smith. *(David Doughty collection)*

Keith Robinson outside Hoyland Cinema,
Market Street, 1952. *(Keith Robinson
collection)*

Lily and Jim Bowley outside their bungalow at 91 Barber Street, 1966. Jim was born on 28 August 1888. Lily died in February 1967 and Jim followed his wife two months later. *(Theresa Whittlestone)*

Taken in the early 1970s, this photograph shows the buildings situated in King Street, below the Queen's Head, which were demolished during Hoyland's massive redevelopment programme. The shiny black sign with white lettering of Hague's butcher's shop can be seen just after the steps, after which is the premises where John Guest and Sons Ltd, pawnbrokers and clothiers, and latterly Derek Bean's antique shop, once stood. *(Keith Robinson collection)*

George and Joan Hopson, landlord and landlady of Hoyland's popular Strafford Arms, at the function organised to mark their retirement, October 1980. *(Joan Hopson)*

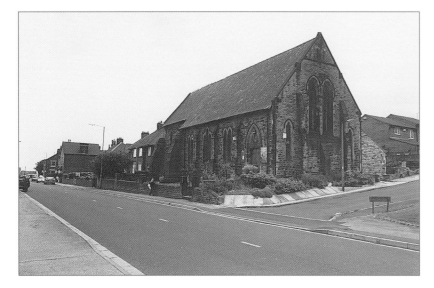

St Andrew's Church and Market Street, July 2000. The church was built on land given by the 6th Earl Fitzwilliam to the designs of local architect Walter John Sykes, of West Bank House. The foundation stone was laid by Countess Fitzwilliam on 23 April 1889. The Earl also gave £200 towards the building costs and Martha Knowles, who owned the grocery store on the corner of Market Street and King Street, contributed £100. The total building costs amounted to £1,348. *(Paul T. Langley Welch)*

High Street, summer 2001. *(Author's collection)*

The junction of King Street with Southgate, summer 2001. This is the start of the one-way system to bypass the town centre, when travelling from Elsecar. On the right can be seen Peter's barber's shop and next door is the double-fronted shop currently occupied by Doreen Law's ladies' and childrens outfitters, which trades from the former business premises of the once well-known Hoyland firm, now defunct, of painters, decorators, plumbers, electricians and glaziers, C. Firth and Sons. These premises were built in 1907. *(Author's collection)*

2
Elsecar through the Years

The EFW flour mill, Wath Road, 1930s. Albert Sylvester made deliveries at this time.
(M. Joan Burgin)

A nineteenth-century view of Wath Road and the Elsecar branch of the Dearne and Dove Canal. On the left is Dallinson's farmhouse. The EFW flour mill can be seen on the right, and in the foreground is one of the many barges that used this once busy canal. Barge traffic ceased in 1911 because cargoes were lost to the Elsecar Branch Railway. The horse-drawn conveyance seen here was later used by the Dallinsons' daughter Gladys to deliver milk around the village, which she continued to do until the Second World War. Gladys Dallinson married Hubert Kay and they lived in The Croft. *(Kevin Cooper)*

The Elsecar branch of the Barnsley British Co-operative Society, seen here during its early years of trading. Edwin Haywood laid the foundation stone of this group of two shops and a dwelling house on 29 October 1892. The grocery department is the double-fronted shop on the left. The Co-op manager's house is in the centre and the single-storey building on the right was the Co-op butcher. However, the butcher's shop closed and was used for storage, possibly because there was stiff competition in the butchery trade in Elsecar, and the Co-op had another butcher's shop nearby in Hoyland. After the Second World War, during the late 1940s, following the retirement of Mr Waring, proprietor of a butcher's shop in Hill Street, the Co-op took over his business and traded from his former premises. *(Keith Robinson collection)*

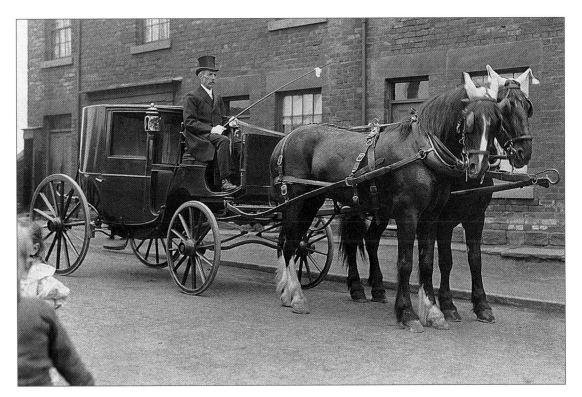

Henry Kelly with his landau
and team at the top of
St Helen's Street, late
nineteenth century.
(Keith Robinson collection)

ST. HELEN'S STREET,
Elsecar, *Aug 31 1911*

Mr C Rowbottom

Dr. to HENRY KELLY,
PROPRIETOR OF
Cabs, Large and Small Waggonettes for Pleasure Parties.
HEARSE AND FUNERAL CARRIAGES.
☞ ORDERS PROMPTLY ATTENDED TO.

A bill to Mr C. Rowbottom from
Henry Kelly of St Helen's
Street, dated 31 August 1911.
The letterhead describes the
diversity of conveyances
Mr Kelly could provide.
(Keith Robinson collection)

Fitzwilliam Street, looking towards the Butchers Arms, early twentieth century. Sadly, some of the properties on the left, built by the Fitzwilliam family during the nineteenth century, had to be demolished in the 1980s, long after the 10th Earl Fitzwilliam had disposed of his Elsecar properties to the local authority. The lost cottages were deemed to be beyond repair because of severe mining subsidence. Once again, thanks for this and other acts of vandalism in Elsecar are owed to the short-sightedness of local decision-makers. The cottages built by the Fitzwilliams that remain are a great asset to Elsecar's appearance. With a little thought, the mistakes of the past could be remedied. It would not be too difficult to rebuild the lost properties in the same style using complementary materials. *(Chris Sharp of Old Barnsley)*

Hill Street, early twentieth century. Left to right: The Manse, Elsecar Congregational Church, and the Royal Oak, popularly known as 'Tommy Upsteps'. *(Edwin Moody collection)*

This early twentieth-century view of Elsecar Congregational Church shows the fine proportions of this popular place of worship, before it succumbed to the ravages of mining subsidence. Its condition was considered so bad that it was demolished and replaced by a new church in the 1980s. *(Edwin Moody collection)*

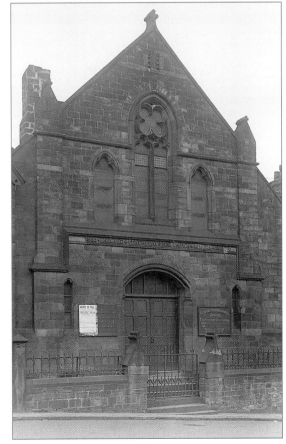

Opposite, bottom: The Fitzwilliam family, notably the 4th, 5th and 6th Earls Fitzwilliam, was responsible for the development of Elsecar as a village from what was still, towards the end of the eighteenth century, just a few scattered farms and cottages. The 4th Earl engaged the fashionable and accomplished architect John Carr (1723–1807), often referred to as Carr of York, to produce designs for cottages to house his colliers. Carr submitted designs for six types. Those which were built include what later became known as Station Row, in Wath Road, and six cottages (two semi-detached between two detached, and eighteenth-century country house lodge-like in appearance) at Skiers Hall. Other cottages, including those seen here, are of a later date than Carr's work. This photograph shows 38, 40 and 42 Fitzwilliam Street, now demolished. *(Keith Robinson collection)*

Wentworth Road and Water Lane, looking towards Mill Lane and the Roundhouse at Barrow (out of sight), taken by F.R. Haigh, 1905. At that time Elsecar Reservoir occupied land on both sides of the bridge. The water on the Wentworth side disappeared when the water level in the reservoir was allowed to drop between the two world wars. *(Keith Robinson collection)*

This F.R. Haigh view shows the bridge over the Dearne and Dove Canal, Elsecar branch, 1905. The chimney belongs to Earl Fitzwilliam's Hemingfield Colliery. How beautiful the countryside was before the pit tip of Elsecar Main obliterated the view. *(Keith Robinson collection)*

An Edwardian view of St Helen's Street. St Helen's Street and the Roman Catholic church built there in 1866 and dedicated to St Helen took their names from the mother of the Roman Emperor Constantine. The church was relocated to West Street, Hoyland, after the Midland Railway Company purchased the site in the 1890s. That church later became part of a school attached to yet another church, built in the Italian Tuscan style and consecrated in 1929. The original church survived for almost a century, being used for various purposes. Today a small housing estate occupies the site of the original church and its grounds. *(Chris Sharp of Old Barnsley)*

John Henry Tollerfield, bailiff, of Pond House, in his boat on Elsecar Reservoir, *c.* 1910. *(David Doughty collection)*

His Majesty King George V at Earl Fitzwilliam's Elsecar Main Colliery, 9 July 1912. Standing next to the King, respectfully doffing his bowler hat, is the 7th Earl Fitzwilliam. *(Edwin Hugh Stenton and Amy Stenton)*

The laying of the foundation stone of Elsecar Midland Working Men's Club, 12 September 1914. *(Edwin Moody collection)*

Albert Backhouse (left), William Penty (right) and an unidentified boy, during the First World War. The cart is pulled by Bob the horse. They are collecting for wounded soldiers outside the group of houses in Elsecar known as the Barracks, which once stood almost opposite Milton Farm. *(Keith Robinson collection)*

Peace celebrations, Fitzwilliam Street. In the background can be seen Ebenezer Place and beyond it Church Street. *(Keith Robinson collection)*

An early view of the Ship Inn, Wath Road. *(Keith Robinson collection)*

Another view of the Ship Inn, as it appeared during its last years before demolition. The eighteenth-century building was demolished between the world wars and replaced by the present brick-built Ship Inn. *(Keith Robinson collection)*

Speights Row, showing a group of lavatories, with Foundry Street behind, 1920s. Speights Row was situated below the Crown Inn, off Fitzwilliam Street and ran parallel to Foundry Street. The dog Lady belonged to Horace Moody, son-in-law of Charlotte Emma Evans, who lived at no. 9. Over forty years after Speights Row was demolished remnants of the buildings still remain in the retaining wall below Foundry Street. *(Edwin Moody collection)*

Charlotte Mary Evans outside her home at 9 Speights Row, *c.* 1925. Houses in Foundry Street can be seen in the background. *(Edwin Moody collection)*

Speights Row, 1927. The widowed Charlotte Emma Evans, mother of Clara Moody, lived at no. 9. Seen here are Horace and Clara Moody. *(Edwin Moody collection)*

Above, left: Speights Row, *c.* 1928. Left to right: Horace Moody, Charlotte Emma Evans, Clara Moody with her son Kenneth on her knee. *(Edwin Moody collection)*

Above, right: The Dell, Elsecar Park, 1929: Clara and Horace Moody with their sons Kenneth (born 1924) and Edwin (born 1920). *(Edwin Moody collection)*

Right: Edwin Moody, Kenneth Moody, Lady and Horace Moody, outside 9 Speights Row, *c.* 1930. The gable seen at the end of the passage belongs to Early's shop, a general grocer in Fitzwilliam Street, just before its junction with Hill Street, formerly known as Stubbin. Speights Row was a row of eleven houses. No. 1 was nearest Fitzwilliam Street. There was an entry between nos 5 and 6 and no. 11 had a kitchen extension. Families living in Speights Row at this time included Mr Samson Vickers and family at no 1 (see page 70). There was an extension facing Fitzwilliam Street, where they had a small confectionery and ice cream shop, later run for many years by Samson's daughter, Alice Potts. At no. 2 lived Annie Littlewood, the Guests lived at no. 4, the Speight family at no. 5, the Spence family at no. 6, George Speight and family at no. 7, Mrs Sellars at no. 8, Charlotte Emma Evans at no. 9, Lewis Widowson at no. 10 and John Penty at no. 11. *(Edwin Moody collection)*

Three Midland Railway Company employees at Elsecar & Hoyland railway station, 24 October 1930: Bill Richardson of Darfield, Graham Ellis of Monk Bretton and Sydney Kirk Walker (1908–88), who then worked as a porter. Sidney Kirk Walker worked for over forty years on the railway and lived in Knollbeck Avenue, Brampton. He finished his working life at Wharncliffe Sidings and retired on 5 June 1970. On 15 June, in recognition of his forty-one years' service, he was presented with a gold watch at Sheaf House, Sheffield, by the Divisional Movements Manager, Mr H. Amos. *(Rex Walker)*

A Whitsuntide parade in Fitzwilliam Street, 1930s. Whitney's farm (Milton Farm) can be seen dominating the centre background. *(Keith Robinson collection)*

A composite postcard showing views around Elsecar, 1930s. *(M. Joan Burgin)*

The official reopening of the EFW flour mill, Wath Road, by Countess Fitzwilliam. The flour mill was refurbished and modernised as part of the celebrations to mark the coming of age of Viscount Milton (born 31 December 1910). Among those featured are, left to right, Colonel J.W.B. Landon (Agent of Earl Fitzwilliam's Wentworth Estate), Lord Milton (in Homburg hat) and Lady Fitzwilliam (centre). *(Roy Young)*

The 'Ocean Wave', Elsecar Park 1933/4. Situated in the top park, this ride was particularly popular. The bandstand, then still in the top park, can be seen in the distance behind it. Pond House is on the right. Dora Cooke is seen here with her daughter Mavis (now Mrs Keith Robinson) and cousin, Frank Clarke. *(Keith Robinson collection)*

Mann's ice cream cart, Elsecar Park, *c.* 1936. About to purchase an ice cream for his daughter Mavis (just visible bottom left) is Allan Cooke. *(Keith Robinson collection)*

This photograph taken at the rear of the Market Place, *c.* 1936, shows, left to right, Mr Evans, Arnold Roberts, Clara Roberts, Mavis Cooke, Dora Cooke, Mrs Evans and Allan Cooke. Mr and Mrs Evans ran the shop in the Market Place at this time. *(Keith Robinson collection)*

Jack Howse and Stanley Nelder at the rear of 3 Wentworth Road, home of Mr and Mrs Isadore Howse and family, Sunday 28 August 1938. The building on the left was the wash house, where the family's laundry was done. *(Doreen Howse collection)*

Elsecar Church of England School, infants class, 1938/9. The teachers are Mrs Oxley, Mrs Hague and Miss Booth. Back row, left to right: on the rocking horse, Brenda Lomas, Mavis Cooke, Yvonne Crow, Eric Siddall and Joy Mallinson (bottom of slide). Middle row: leaning on the elephant, Dennis Leathers, Peter Galloway, Doris Green (left-hand side of see-saw), Clifford Parkin, Shirley Beardshall (right-hand side of see-saw), Brian Siddall, Maureen Sokell, Maurice Hector and Georgie Jones. Front row: Vera Callea, David Cooke, Janet Burgin, Billie Crossland, Frank Stevenson, Freda Jones and Donald Mallinson. *(Keith Robinson collection)*

Tom Hill and his sons outside the EFW flour mill, Elsecar, during Second World War. Left to right: The youngest son, Harry (1915–66), engineer, who worked in Sheffield at Millspaugh Ltd; Tom Hill (1872–1954), who worked for Earl Fitzwilliam's Wentworth Estates, as cashier at the Estate Office, for fifty years, and lived at 25 Clayfields Lane, Wentworth (there is a bench in Clayfields Lane, dedicated to his memory); Tom Rowland (1907–81), the eldest son, manager of the EFW flour mill, seen here in his warden's uniform; and Tom Hill's second son Geoff (1911–74), an architect who worked for Wombwell UDC. *(M. Joan Burgin)*

Miss Mary Senior (born 1923), in her ATS uniform. Mary worked as a shorthand typist. She was stationed at Pontefract, Glasgow and finally Bradford. She was given the rank of corporal and her principal function was to be in attendance at court martials. *(Mary Fenton)*

The Fenton brothers on the doorstep of 6 Vizard Road, Elsecar, in the late 1940s. Left to right, Gordon, Jack and Alan. *(Mary Fenton)*

Jack and Mary Fenton, seen here in April 1952 in the garden of their home at 6 Vizard Road, with their baby daughter Kathleen, who had been christened that morning. Kathleen was born on 8 March. The Fenton family later moved to Parkside Road, Hoyland Common. In 1971 the Fentons purchased Station House, 9 Wath Road, Elsecar, the former stationmaster's house (for the freight line and the Fitzwilliam private railway station), from Earl Fitzwilliam's (Wentworth) Estates. *(Mary Fenton)*

Jack Fenton (1922–88). When young, Jack lived at 109 Strafford Avenue, Elsecar. He began working at Elsecar Workshops, which in the days before nationalisation of the coal industry was still owned by Earl Fitzwilliam. His work was building wooden wagons. He subsequently moved to Manvers Main, where he inspected wagons, a job he remained in until his retirement. On 26 March 1946 Jack Fenton married Corporal Mary Senior ATS, daughter of Mr and Mrs William Senior of Spring Gardens, Hoyland. *(Mary Fenton)*

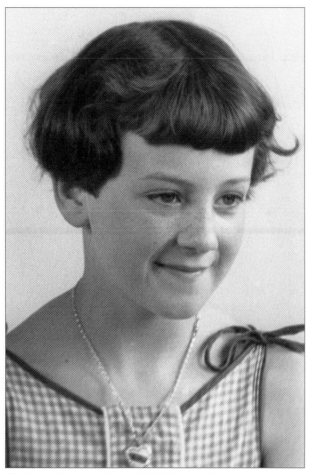

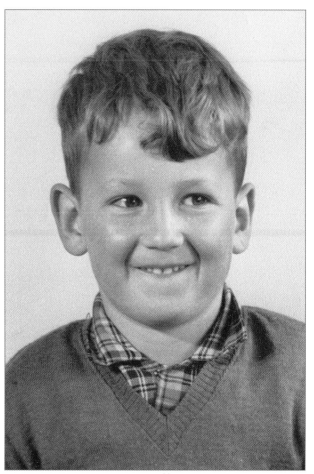

Kathleen Fenton (born 1952), daughter of Jack and Mary Fenton, of Vizard Road. *(Mary Fenton)*

David Fenton (born 1943), son of Jack and Mary Fenton, while a pupil at King Street School. He now lives in High Green and works for Fletcher's Bakeries. *(Mary Fenton)*

Some well-known Elsecar residents, 1940s. Back row, left to right: Leonard (Len) Loy snr, Sam Wood, Issy (Isadore) Howse, Bill Chadwick (of Distillery Side), and Horace Thickett (landlord of the Market Hotel). Front row: Alwyn Evans, W. Townsend and A. Teague. *(Brenda Loy)*

Elsecar combined churches Sunday School queen, Margaret Falding (now Mrs Turner), Whitsuntide 1946. Margaret was from Holy Trinity Church. She was the first Sunday School queen after the Second World War. *(Edwin Moody collection)*

Mavis Cooke in Fitzwilliam Street, 1940s. Peering over the wall is her father Allan. The Crown Garage can be seen in the background. *(Keith Robinson collection)*

An aerial view of Wath Road, c. 1950. It shows the Dearne and Dove Canal (in the foreground), the EFW flour mill (left centre foreground), the Ship Inn, Meadow Row, Reform Row and St John's Methodist Chapel. Note the allotments, which in the decade that followed would be occupied by Gray Street. *(M. Joan Burgin)*

The 'Congs' school room, Elsecar Congregational Church, Hill Street, late 1940s or early 1950s. Among those pictured are Horace Moody, Walter Wigfield, Iris Bamforth, Myra Power, Mrs Massingham, Mrs John Noble, Mrs Popplewell, Mrs Goddard, Mrs Walker, Malcolm Scott, Robert Popplewell, Russell Moody, George Moody, Joe Scott, John Bowden, Fred Swallow, Peter Ashwell, James Massingham, John Noble, Mrs Power, Mrs Hanstock, Mrs Mary Scott, Mrs Russell Moody, Mrs Fred Swallow, Mrs Horace Moody, Mrs Billie Naylor, Mrs Greenfield and Margaret Noble. *(Edwin Moody collection)*

Elsecar Congregational Church, 1950s. Left to right: Mrs Russell Moody, Mrs Horace Moody, Mrs William Naylor, Mrs Walker (of Howse Street), Miss Mary Naylor (later Mrs Billy Walker) and Mrs John Noble. *(Edwin Moody collection)*

The Lewis family. The Lewises came from Burnham-on-Sea in Somerset. Mr Lewis was Minister of Wombwell and Elsecar Congregational Churches during the 1950s and 1960s. The family lived in Armroyd Lane. Mr and Mrs Lewis are pictured here with their daughter Olwyn and their son Kerri. *(Edwin Moody collection)*

Ebenezer Place, 1960. Left to right: Marilyn Thrush, Christine Howse, Anne Stewart, Graham Wood and, holding Paul Bostwick on his knee, Ian Stewart. *(Christine Walker)*

Anne Fletcher outside 10 Tomlinson Road. Built after the Second World War and first occupied towards the end of the 1940s, the prefabs, one of which is seen here, provided comfortable, spacious accommodation for many Elsecar and Hoyland families. They were equipped with every modern convenience, which included American-style fitted kitchens with a built-in cooker and refrigerator, and a bathroom with wash basin, bath and lavatory. Indoor conveniences, let alone bathrooms, were then still a rarity in many properties throughout the area. The prefabs served a very useful housing need and were generally highly regarded by the people who lived there.

The largest building project undertaken in its final years by the much-lamented Hoyland Urban District Council, which became defunct in 1974, was the building of the Cloughfields Estate. Many residents in the prefabs, including those in Tomlinson Road, which linked the Hoyland part of Cherry Tree Street with Elsecar, Neild Road, Bevan Close and Vizard Road, which ran from the end of Wentworth Road at its junction with Cobcar Lane along Jump Valley, were moved to the new estate. As families were decanted to The Cloughs, prefabs were demolished. The remaining prefabs in Tomlinson Road were finally demolished in 1973. Some in Wood View and Zetland Road, Elsecar, survived into the 1980s and others in Tinker Lane, Hoyland Common, still stand today, although they have been clad in brick. *(Theresa Whittlestone)*

Outside the loco shed at Elsecar Main Colliery, *c.* 1964. Left to right: Harry Porter (driver), Rex Walker, crouching inside locomotive (shunter), Ernest Tomlinson (foreman of the boiler house) and Geoff Swallow, who worked in the fitting shop. In the background can be seen Turner's Garage in Wath Road and Reform Row. *(Rex Walker)*

Some of Hoyland and district's business community at a function held at the Milton Hall by Hoyland and District Road Haulage Association, *c.* 1969. Among those included here are: Mr and Mrs Les Webster, Derek Bean and Dot Bean, David and Christine Walker and John and Marjorie Green. *(David and Christine Walker)*

Theresa Fletcher in the front garden of 10 Tomlinson Road, 1972. Part of Jump can be seen in the background. This is one of the last photographs taken of the prefabs in Tomlinson Road before the remaining residents were moved to the Cloughfields Estate. *(Theresa Whittlestone)*

Two young ladies sharing a joke with well-known comedian Charlie Williams at the Crown Inn, 1972. On the left is Denise Egbury and on the right is Wilma Gourley. *(Mary Fenton)*

The EFW flour mill, after it was sold to Elsecar Stone Ground Flour Mills, late 1960s. *(M. Joan Burgin)*

Roland Hill and Gary Mallinson at work in the EFW flour mill. *(M. Joan Burgin)*

The top floor of the EFW flour mill.
(M. Joan Burgin)

The middle floor of the EFW flour mill.
(M. Joan Burgin)

The basement of the EFW flour mill.
(M. Joan Burgin)

The weighing room on the top floor of the EFW flour mill. Filled 3lb bags of EFW stoneground flour can be seen on the bench. *(M. Joan Burgin)*

J. Davy and Co. Ltd was founded in 1869 by Jonathan Davy and run by four generations of the family until its closure on 23 May 1980. This photograph, taken on 21 May 1980, at Davy's Foundry, Foundry Street, shows, from left to right, Vin Preston, Bill Rowbottom, R. Bagley, Donald Doughty, T. Brack, Gordon Whitehouse, Jimmy Wroe, D. Foster, P. Oliver, Mrs Molly Davy and Mr Ryan Davy. *(Keith Robinson collection)*

Hill Street from the junction of Wilkinson Road, July 2000. Evans Terrace stood on the green where the trees have been planted until the early 1960s. The distinctive spire of Holy Trinity Church, Wentworth, can be seen on the horizon. *(Paul T. Langley Welch)*

Hill Street at its junction with Fitzwilliam Street, Church Street and Foundry, December 2000. The Barracks (see page 28) were situated in Fitzwilliam Street on the left-hand side, adjacent to the first cottage seen here. This cottage was once the home of Jimmy Barraclough, the dancing teacher (see page 97). *(Author)*

A view from the end of Church Street, looking across Fitzwilliam Street, December 2000. The bungalow in the centre was built on the site of Samson Vickers shop (see page 70), after Speights Row was pulled down in the 1960s. The building on the left was for many years a butcher's shop attached to Milton Farm and run by Guests. It is the only part of the farm (for many years occupied by the Whitney family) still standing. The former butcher's shop is presently being run as a take-away sandwich shop. *(Author)*

3
Areas in &
Around Hoyland

Some of the area's older residents rest for a few
moments on the bench placed by George Palmer
conveniently near his home, Milton Cottage, Palmers
Hill, 1930s. *(Kevin Cooper)*

F.P. 38. Milton Pottery, Hoyland

Milton Pottery, *c.* 1912. Earl Fitzwilliam's Milton Pottery was situated at Skiers Spring, near the brickworks. It operated from 1911 to 1931 and specialised in the production of pancheons, bread pots, plant pots and utilitarian household items. Two brothers named Keir came from Cumbria to run the pottery. *(Edwin Moody collection)*

As well as producing items for export outside the area, Milton Pottery made goods to order for anyone who made a personal call at the works. The Potters Wheel, a public house on the Cloughfields Estate, was named to commemorate Milton Pottery. Pictured here are some of the staff at Milton Pottery displaying a selection of the wares produced there. *(Edwin Moody collection)*

Skiers Spring drift mine and shaft. This colliery closed in 1976. *(David Doughty collection)*

The pithead baths, Skiers Spring drift mine. *(David Doughty collection)*

A pre-nationalisation LNER South Yorkshire Pullman train at Skiers Spring. *(Keith Robinson collection)*

A very rare and interesting view showing the Cat and Dog Pond on Milton Forge and buildings in Milton Road and Millhouses Street. The Cat and Dog Pond (so called because many unwanted pets had been disposed of there) was one of five ponds which once existed near the site of Milton Iron Works, which closed on 31 January 1884. It was filled in in the 1940s. Another pond had previously been filled in, in 1930. This pond stood on the opposite side of Millhouses Street near the junction of Milton Road. The three-storey mill house, from which Millhouses Street takes its name, can just be seen: it is the last building on the right in the centre of the photograph. The site of the mill house is now occupied by modern bungalows built by W. Chadwick and Son in the 1960s. The mill pond was filled in by Hoyland UDC in order to build Wentworth View and Milton Crescent and the old people's bungalows in Millhouses Street itself. Only two ponds remain today. A third, adjacent to Milton Road, was filled in by Hoyland UDC in 1965, when the site was used as a refuse tip. The building with the chimney seen here, which formed part of the iron works complex, was used by Hoyland UDC as an incinerator, known as the 'destructor'. (*Kevin Cooper*)

Wombwell Road, Platts Common, 1930. Left to right: Lily Bowley, Prince, Roy Fletcher and Bess. (*Theresa Whittlestone*)

David Hornsby, one-time lodger of Roy and Anne Fletcher, seen here in his Ford 8, 1936. *(Theresa Whittlestone)*

The junction of Barnsley Road with Wentworth Road, Blacker Hill, early twentieth century. The Royal Albert Hotel, the only public house to remain open in Blacker Hill today, is on the left. The Mission Hall, which served as the village community centre and stood adjacent to Blacker Hill chapel, can be seen in the centre background. *(Chris Sharp of Old Barnsley)*

An early twentieth-century view of Wentworth Road, Blacker Hill, facing in the opposite direction to the view above. Blacker Hill post office is in the left foreground, the Blacksmith's Arms is next to it and a little further down the street is the Travellers. Across the road is Blacker Hill Working Men's Club. *(Chris Sharp of Old Barnsley)*

An aerial view of Hoyland Brick Co. Ltd, 1959. The Barnsley (Courthouse station) to Sheffield (Great Central) railway line can be seen, and beyond it the single Derby line to Rockingham and Wharncliffe Silkstone collieries. *(David Doughty collection)*

Terry Gallagher, outside the offices of Hoyland Marshall, 1990. This was the former Hoyland Brick Co. Ltd, which became a subsidiary of Thomas Marshall and Co. Ltd of Loxley in 1957. The works was eventually renamed Hoyland Marshall. *(Terry Gallagher)*

Metalliform came to Hoyland Common from Leeds in 1946, and opened a factory in the dance hall/cinema known as 'Old Staggy's' in Central Street. This view of Metalliform from the junction of Central Street in 1914 shows, from left to right, Joyce Parrot, Carol Mallinson and Terry Gallagher. *(Terry Gallagher)*

St Peter's Church, Tankersley, October 1982. The church has its origins in the tenth century, although apart from two pieces of stonework nothing remains of the Saxon structure. Of more recent additions, the chancel is the oldest part of the church and dates from the early thirteenth century. The tower is Perpendicular but with the exception of the late sixteenth-century clerestory and the north aisle, which was rebuilt in 1881, most of the rest is Decorated. Nothing remains of the ancient stained glass of which some records remain but there is some fine stained glass in the nave. Known as the Walker windows, they were designed by Edward Burne-Jones and date from 1879. The porch, which has more ancient origins, was repaired and reconstructed in 1726 and again in 1881. Set into the interior walls are fragments of stone coffin lids from the twelfth and thirteenth centuries. The porch gate was designed by Sir Edwin Lutyens in 1901. An annual ceremony takes place on the second Sunday following 29 June (St Peter's Day). Known as *ycleppings*, it was reintroduced to Tankersley during the 1920s by Canon Douglas. Its origins date from long before a church stood in Tankersley. Traditionally it involves parishioners holding hands, forming a ring around the church and embracing it – yclepping – the object being to create a force against evil. In the churchyard are some gravestones dating from the seventeenth century, but some of the most interesting date from the nineteenth, and include memorials to many well-known local industrialists such as members of the Chambers family. *(Terry Gallagher and Robert Henry Mower)*

St Peter's Church, Tankersley: the chancel viewed from the nave, 1982. The rood loft and its staircase, just visible on the right, were built with the nave. The loft was uncovered and restored by Canon Douglas, who was rector of Tankersley from 1918 to 1942, a noted historian and antiquarian. He added the rood screen and the choir stalls in 1922. Despite the church's age wall monuments are surprisingly few. Some may have been taken down and others covered by the thick rendering, which obscures what features remain on the interior walls. The box pews were removed during rebuilding work between 1879 and 1881, when the north aisle (known as the Eland aisle) was enlarged and replaced with the present pews, raised on wooden plinths. This has, together with thick carpeting, obscured any remaining floor monuments. There are one or two exceptions including the tombstone in the chancel of 'Thomas Toytill, Priest', who was at one time Chaplain of St Peter's, and died on 28 April 1492. A memorial to Ann Fanshaw who died in 1654, sited near the pulpit, is no longer visible, although it still features in the church's guide-book, published in 1983. On the west wall in a glass case are some cannon balls. They were found nearby and are from the Battle of Tankersley Moor of 1643, one of the minor skirmishes which took place during the Civil War. St Peter's has a pleasing ambience and a large congregation as well as an excellent choir. *(Terry Gallagher and Robert Henry Mower)*

Birdwell Common at the junction of The Walk with Sheffield Road, early twentieth century. *(Chris Sharp of Old Barnsley)*

Whitsuntide Parade in Chapel Street, Birdwell, early twentieth century. Notice the harmonium on the trap. *(David Doughty collection)*

Birdwell Methodist Chapel, Chapel Street, Birdwell, 12 January 1938. In the photograph are Mrs Brammah and son, Mrs Marsh, Ernest Marsh, Edith Doughty, David Doughty, Mrs Ridgeway and Gordon Ridgeway. *(David Doughty collection)*

Wentworth Street, Birdwell. The large building (middle left) is the Barnsley British Co-operative store. The house sticking out into the road (with gable end showing) is the school caretaker's house. Both the school and the caretaker's house were demolished in the mid-1950s. *(David Doughty collection)*

Mounted troops in Wentworth Park during the Great Coal Strike of 1893. Pictured are four squadrons of dragoons and just visible on the extreme right, one squadron of lancers. Troops were billeted in the stable block, but it was actually not necessary to defend Earl Fitzwilliam and Wentworth Woodhouse. This was because, although he and his predecessors had steadfastly forbidden their miners to be members of a union, the wages paid and fringe benefits received meant that the miners in the employ of the Earl were already considerably better off than miners elsewhere. However, miners who dissented were summarily dismissed. Strikes in Fitzwilliam-owned collieries had been rare but along with all other collieries in South Yorkshire, the great stoppage of July–November 1893 closed them all. *(Roy Young)*

The statement issued by Lord Fitzwilliam following the 1893 Great Coal Strike. *(Edwin Hugh Stenton and Amy Stenton)*

To my Workmen at Low Stubbin and Elsecar.

I am informed that you have applied to Mr. Newbould to be re-engaged as my workmen, but before I can give any reply to that request I wish to lay some considerations before you.

I have always refused to belong to any association or federation which might fetter me in my dealings with my workmen ; and I wish to secure for them the same absolute freedom to be or not to be members of any association or federation as they think best.

There have been no difficulties or differences between us respecting wages ; I believe you had no cause for complaint ; so that I am at a loss to know why you laid my pits idle.

So late as the 25th of July last I had the pleasure of seeing you all at my house and receiving a most gratifying proof of your kindly feeling and good will towards me and mine ; and among my most valued possessions is a beautiful book which you gave me. In it are inscribed the names and length of service of all who were in my employment. There I see that many had worked 20, some 30, and some even 50 years and more for me and for my father before me.

Such ties as these create strong regard on both sides and are not easily broken.

I am therefore driven to believe that it was intimidation only which caused you to leave your work ; and those who led you to do so are responsible for the whole of the suffering which you and your families have endured for so long, and also for the want and misery of so many others who have been thrown out of work by your action.

There will always be differences of opinion among men, but if we can bear in mind the Divine command " to do unto others as we would they should do unto us " those differences will never assume any formidable dimensions.

There cannot be a more false or dangerous doctrine than the belief that the interests of employer and employed are opposed to each other. Their real interests must always be one and the same, and they must stand or fall together.

If my pits are re-opened it must be on the understanding that there is an entire absence of intimidation among my workmen, and that they will not interfere with each other whether they are or are not members of any federation.

I am too far off to have an interview with you myself, but if you can satisfy my representatives that there shall be absolute freedom for you all, I shall gladly welcome back to my employment as many as possible.

Yours faithfully,

(Signed), FITZWILLIAM.

Coollattin,
        24th Nov., 1893.

The junction of Church Field Lane, The Barrow, Barrow Field Lane and Main Street, from Main Street, Wentworth, pre-1912. *(Chris Sharp of Old Barnsley)*

The stable block, Wentworth Woodhouse, 1910. Seen here are the 7th Earl Fitzwilliam's motor cars. Three of them were manufactured in Sheffield, and are different models of the Simplex marque, designed in the stable block at Wentworth Woodhouse. In 1906 Lord Fitzwilliam offered a plot of his land in Sheffield to the Brotherhood-Crocker Car Company, to build a manufacturing plant to make motor cars. It opened in 1908 and was known as the Simplex Motor Works Ltd. Lord Fitzwilliam was the major shareholder. Various models were made there until 1925; the last, a 50 hp model, was built for the Earl's private use (see page 80). That motor car spent some time at Wentworth before being taken to Ireland to the Fitzwilliams' Coollattin Estate. It was sold in the 1960s and now forms part of the collection at Kelham Island Museum in Sheffield. *(Roy Young)*

The royal luggage arrives at Wentworth Woodhouse prior to the visit of their Majesties King George V and Queen Mary, July 1912. *(Roy Young)*

The male indoor staff at Wentworth Woodhouse, 1912. Back row, left to right: A footman, under butler, Arthur Collier (odd man), William Bristow (footman) and three unknown footmen. Front row: William May (butler), Charles Laughty (groom of the chambers), Sam Gorton (house steward). *(Roy Young)*

Occupation Road, Harley, early twentieth century. *(Chris Sharp of Old Barnsley)*

Harley post office, Harley Road, seen here before the First
World War. *(Chris Sharp of Old Barnsley)*

An early twentieth-century view of The Horseshoe Inn,
Harley, believed to show Mr and Mrs William Heathcote,
landlord and landlady. *(Chris Sharp of Old Barnsley)*

Fund-raising events were common occurrences throughout South Yorkshire during the First World War. This one, organised for the benefit of the Soldiers' Cheer Fund, shows the parade in Hemingfield on 10 July 1915. *(Chris Sharp of Old Barnsley)*

The Milton Arms Hotel, Cemetery Road, Hemingfield, early twentieth century. It was built during the last quarter of the nineteenth century and named in honour of the heir to the Fitzwilliam earldom. There have been six holders of that title since the 4th Earl inherited his uncle's (the 2nd Marquess of Rockingham's) Wentworth estates in 1782. The Milton Arms was closed and boarded up for many years but reopened in the 1980s with a new name, the Fiddlers Inn. Within the last year its new owners have named it the Marbrook Tavern. *(Chris Sharp of Old Barnsley)*

Roy Fletcher, aged one, doing a spot of gardening, Pitt Row, Hemingfield, 1959. *(Theresa Whittlestone)*

Outside 3 Pitt Row, Hemingfield 1963. Back row: Anne Cooper and Gilbert Cooper. Front row: Roy Fletcher and Shaun Fletcher. *(Theresa Whittlestone)*

The colliery tips of Elsecar Main, a popular spot for walkers and young playmates. Seen here on the pit stacks above Pitt Row, Hemingfield, are Shaun Fletcher, Rebel the dog and Roy Fletcher. The dog belonged to Margaret Wright, one of the residents of Pitt Row. *(Theresa Whitlestone)*

The fire-fighting team at Newton Chambers & Co. Ltd, late 1950s. Back row, left to right: Roy Mansfield, Alan Hewling, -?-, -?-, -?-, Brian Wadsworth, Ben Morton, Cliff Jubb, Albert Philips, -?-, -?-. Front row: -?-, Harold Short, -?-, Eric Almond, Gordon Hindley, Ernest Wood. *(Harold Short)*

The Newton Chambers fire-fighting team giving a demonstration in the late 1950s. *(Harold Short)*

St Mary's Church, Worsborough, early twentieth century. Built of local sandstone, it is an unusual-looking building, with a large, almost square nave and aisles. St Mary's has a thin Decorated tower, which has a Perpendicular top and spire. Some Norman work exists in the chancel and its arch to the nave. There is a fifteenth-century roof to the porch which protects the very fine oak door, dating from about 1480. The church also has a Perpendicular chancel screen. Inside are several interesting monuments, including that of Sir Roger Rockley, who died in 1533. This famous double-decker tomb is carved from oak. In repose on the upper deck is a young man in armour. On the lower deck is a skeleton. The base of the tomb bears the arms of Rockley and Mountenay. An inscription, which was fortunately recorded before it disappeared in the mists of time, read: 'Here lies Roger Rockley, knight, son of Thomas Rockley, knight.' There are several other tombs and monuments to members of the Rockley family, who once resided at nearby Worsborough Hall, and to other notable local families including the Elmhirsts, a family associated with the history of this corner of South Yorkshire from at least as early as the late thirteenth century. Members of the family still live nearby at the historic country house Hound Hill. *(Chris Sharp of Old Barnsley)*

Opposite, above: Warren Lane Chapel, Chapeltown, 1936. Included in the photograph are: William Hill (chapel superintendent), Harold Platts, Millie Hill, Nellie Armitage, Joyce Parkin, Sheila Lee, Edith Bowyer, Betty Kilner, Joan Sharpe, Eva Lambert, Elsie Wilkinson, Rene Clarke, Olive Smart, Mary Pepper, Annie Newbold, Nellie Bassinder, Gladys Stutchbury, Gladys Marshall, Maisie Bond, Connie Newbould, Mrs Fisher, Grace Stutchbury, Mrs Chapman, Harry Renshaw (conductor) Harry Evans (headmaster at Warren School), Hilda Mellor, Mrs Crooks, Mary Giles, Emma Moxon, Mrs Hoyland, May Galloway, Isaac Hill and Fred Lambert. *(Joan Hopson)*

Below: The crowning of the anniversary queen, Warren Lane Chapel, Chapeltown, 1952. Jean Goddard is crowned by Mrs Barraclough (previously Miss Moulding and wife of Chapeltown's Dr Barraclough). Also in the photograph are Rosemary Harrison, Catherine Hindley, Carol Hopson, Pat Waite, Miss Denton and pageboy Robert Waite. *(Joan Hopson)*

Situated in what is now known as Worsborough Country Park on the outskirts of Worsborough village, Rockley Hall, once a grand mansion, is seen here in the early twentieth century after its role as a home for the gentry had been downgraded, and it had become just another farmhouse, in need of repair. Now usually referred to as Rockley Old Hall, the major portion of this many-gabled country house dates from the sixteenth century. It continued to be used as a farmhouse until it was divided into several separate dwellings in the 1970s. Since then the hall's occupants have included footballing legend Jack Charlton, during his tenure as manager of Sheffield Wednesday, and the actress Kathy Staff, best known for her appearances in the television programmes *Crossroads*, both the original screening of the soap opera, with its celebrated shaking sets, and its recent revival; *Open All Hours*, which starred Ronnie Barker and David Jason; and the long-running *Last of the Summer Wine*, where her character Nora Batty has become one of the most popular on British television. *(Chris Sharp of Old Barnsley)*

4
Some Notable Personalities

Charles Pitchford, appointed bellman and pindar (poet and storyteller) by Hoyland Local Board
in May 1891. *(Cyril Slinn)*

Joseph Hunter FSA (1783–1861), pictured in the early nineteenth century. This distinguished antiquary and cleric was born in Sheffield, where his father was engaged in the cutlery industry. His mother died when he was young and he was placed under the guardianship of Joseph Evans, a Presbyterian minister. He sent him to school near Sheffield where he received the rudiments of a classical education. The young Joseph Hunter devoted his spare time to antiquarian studies and the collection of church notes. In 1806 he went to York to study for the Presbyterian ministry, and in 1809 became minister of a Presbyterian congregation at Bath, where he resided for twenty-four years. In 1815 he married Mary Hayward, daughter of Francis Hayward MD of Bath, by whom he had six children. In addition to his pastoral duties he continued to add to his collection of books, documents and manuscripts, which enabled him to produce his *Hallamshire*, published in 1819. Two volumes of the *History of the Deanery of Doncaster* followed this in 1828 and 1831. These volumes form the basis of study for many local historians, because they preserve the contents of manuscripts that no longer exist. In volume two he covers, among other subjects, the parish of Wath-upon-Dearne. On page 78 he begins his entry for Wentworth: 'Of all the townships which compose the parish of Wath this has the most splendid destiny.' On page 100 his passage about Hoyland begins: 'Last of the townships which compose the parish of Wath may be placed Hoyland, which is very remote from the parish church, and on the extreme verge of the wapentake of Strafford towards Staincross.' *(Author's collection)*

On his appointment as a sub-commissioner for the Record Commission in 1833, Joseph Hunter moved to London. In this field his contribution is still acknowledged. He spent the rest of his life improving and extending the public record system, becoming an assistant keeper of public records (first class) in 1838 when the Public Record Office was set up. As well as producing many important publications he continued his work as an antiquarian, and his extensive writing included studies of Shakespeare and Pope. He also produced a tract about Robin Hood, setting out to prove that he was a real person. He died in Torrington Square, London, on 9 May 1861 and was interred in the churchyard of St Mary's Church, Ecclesfield, a spot he had chosen for himself because his forefathers lay there. This is his grave. *(Paul T. Langley Welch)*

The Revd Walter Ruthven Pym (1856–1908), Vicar of Wentworth between 1884 and 1889. He was born in Great Chesterford, Essex, into the prosperous landed family descended from John Pym, the great Earl of Strafford's most ardent adversary. Thomas Wentworth, 1st Earl of Strafford (1593–1641), chief minister of King Charles I, was the son of Sir William Wentworth Bt of Wentworth Woodhouse. Strafford was 'murdered by the sword of justice' when he was executed by Parliament's Act of Attainder, unscrupulously obtained, mainly at the instigation of John Pym. Walter Pym's arrival at Wentworth saw a number of changes, which included establishing the church magazine. He was enthusiastically involved in some of the village's sporting activities, which included cricket and football. He left Wentworth for an urban parish, St Andrew's, Sharrow, Sheffield, and then the parish of All Saints, Rotherham. In 1898 he was consecrated Bishop of Mauritius, and in 1903 became Bishop of Bombay. *(Roy Young)*

James Thorley of Alderthwaite and Skiers Spring Lodge (1868–1932), a well-known tenant farmer on Earl Fitzwilliam's Wentworth Estates. Alderthwaite Farm, once a hamlet, is along with Skiers an historic area within the Hoyland district. *(Keith Robinson collection)*

Haymaking at Alderthwaite farm during the early twentieth century. *(Keith Robinson collection)*

Samson Vickers and his puppets, 1920s. This well-known Elsecar resident and confectioner was born in the mid-nineteenth century and lived at 1 Speights Row. He often appeared as an entertainer at local events and was the father of another well-known local resident, Mrs Alice Potts. She took over her father's shop in Fitzwilliam Street adjacent to her father's house, on his retirement. Mrs Potts later lived in Gill Street, Hoyland. *(Kevin Cooper)*

Albert Modley was a cousin of Lily Bowley, who originally came from the Racecommon Road area of Barnsley. He found fame as a comedian, actor and radio personality and was a regular visitor to the Bowleys' home in Hoyland. After his retirement Albert went to live in Lancaster but did the occasional acting engagement. One of his last appearances was in the popular television programme *Tales of the Unexpected* in 1979. *(Theresa Whittlestone)*

Albert Modley worked with the famous BBC radio personality Wilfred Pickles, who had a popular radio show, *Have a Go*, which featured Violet Carson as the pianist (she later played Ena Sharples in *Coronation Street*). The show involved visiting various factories and awarding prizes – 5 bob (25 pence in today's money, but enough to pay for more than a gallon of beer at that time) for a correct answer and £1 for three correct answers. Barney Colehan was also on *Have a Go* and one of Wilfred Pickles' catchphrases was 'Give him the money, Barney'. Seen here in 1944 during a performance are, left to right, Albert Modley, Wilfred Pickles and Barney Colehan. *(Theresa Whittlestone)*

Sir Thomas Tomlinson Kt, BEM, JP (1877–1959). Tommy Tomlinson, as he was affectionately known locally in the years before his knighthood, was one of the area's best-known residents for over forty years. He had an outstanding record of public service. Born on 27 January 1877, the son of William and Ruth Tomlinson, he was educated at Elsecar Church of England School, which he left at the age of twelve to work at Cortonwood Colliery. In 1899 he married my great-grandmother's niece, Alice Hirst, by whom he had a son and daughter. From 1892 to 1906 he worked at the Old Lidgett Colliery, where he spent fourteen years as a dataller. In 1906 he went to Earl Fitzwilliam's Hemingfield Colliery also as a dataller. From 1913 until he resigned in 1952 he worked as checkweighman at Elsecar Main Colliery. In 1910 Tommy Tomlinson became branch secretary of the YMA (Yorkshire Miners' Association). In 1912 he was elected to Hoyland UDC for the Elsecar Ward, which he represented for the next twenty-four years. He was made a Justice of the Peace in 1919. In 1920 he was Chairman of Hoyland UDC and also of the education committee. That same year he also became a member of the advisory committee to the Lord Lieutenant of the county. In 1921 Tommy Tomlinson was elected to the County Council and in 1922 he became a member of the Miners' Welfare Commission. In 1924 he was representative of the WRCC (West Riding County Council) to the County Council Association and was also appointed to the Joint Wages Board of the YMA. He became an alderman in 1929, and continued as a member of Hoyland UDC until 1940, serving as Chairman in 1921–3 and 1933–5. In 1943 he became a member of the Board of Mining Examiners and also of the National Free Church Council Executive. He was awarded the BEM (British Empire Medal) in 1945. From 1945–6 he was president of the Wesleyan Reform Union and from 1946–9 and 1952–5 chairman of the West Riding County Council. Tommy Tomlinson was knighted in 1954. His other activities included serving as a lay preacher for over fifty years and being a Sunday School teacher. He was also proprietor of the Crown Garage in Fitzwilliam Street (see page 38), which was later taken over by Jack Oxley. He was a major figure at the Wesleyan Reform Church, Church Street, Elsecar, which was near his family home. Sir Thomas and Lady Tomlinson lived in one of Earl Fitzwilliam's cottages at 20 Fitzwilliam Street, Elsecar, and their easily memorised telephone number was Hoyland 2221.

This photograph was taken in the garden of Sir Thomas's daughter (Minnie Wood) in The Croft, Elsecar. Back row: Minnie Wood and her husband Harry. Minnie died aged seventy-nine on 19 April 1979 and Harry aged eighty-six on 6 December 1985. On the left of the front row is Barbara Tomlinson (born 31 August 1942, now Mrs Mellar), granddaughter of Sir Thomas and Alice, Lady Tomlinson and youngest daughter of Ernest Tomlinson (Sir Thomas died on 11 February 1957, aged eighty; Alice died on 5 March 1963, aged eighty-two). On the right is Janet Tomlinson, great-granddaughter of Sir Thomas and Lady Tomlinson, daughter of Wilf Tomlinson (son of Sir Thomas's son Ernest) and niece of Barbara Tomlinson, the other little girl pictured. *(Herbert and Doreen Howse)*

The Imperial Society of Knights Bachelor

Know all men by these Presents that Her Majesty's Secretary of State for the Home Department having notified unto this Society that on the Sixth day of July, One thousand nine hundred and fifty-four, Her Majesty was pleased to confer the Dignity of Knighthood upon

THOMAS TOMLINSON, Esq., B.E.M.

In consequence and pursuance thereof the said

SIR THOMAS TOMLINSON

has been admitted to be a Member of the Imperial Society of Knights Bachelor and is duly entered in the Society's Roll. In testimony whereof the Seal of the said Society is affixed to this Certificate the same being duly attested by us.

_____
Knight Principal

- - - - - - - - - - - - - - - - - -
Registrar.

A certificate with citation of Sir Thomas Tomlinson. *(Ian J. Stewart)*

Isaac Lichmere Walker (1885–1958), seen here as President of Hoyland and District Chamber of Trade, during his tenure of office, 1950–1. Lichie Walker, as he was invariably known, was the son of a Barnsley newsagent. He married Annetta Crowe (1886–1969) of Wombwell in 1911 and set up business in Hoyland as a confectioner. He later took over his aunt's newsagency at 8 King Street and transferred his business to larger premises at 22 High Street in the early 1930s. He built the large house known as Arrandale in West Street, where he and his wife lived until their deaths. The Walkers had a son, Geoffrey, born in 1914 and a daughter, Joan, born in 1916. The family business continues, having being run by his son Geoff (1914–95) and currently by Lichie's grandson David and his wife Christine, in enlarged premises at 22–4 High Street, Hoyland. *(Ralph Walker)*

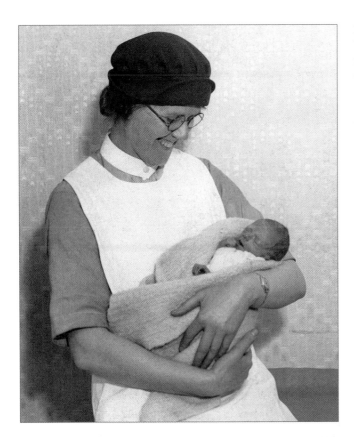

Nora Walker (1899–1989). Nurse Walker, Elsecar's popular midwife, lived in a cottage at Skiers Hall. She was the daughter of Thomas Walker (1867–1948), famous locally for his coal carvings. During her long career, Nurse Walker delivered 4,997 babies. She is seen here during the 1920s. *(Keith Robinson collection)*

George Palmer (1904–83), lived at Milton Cottage, Palmers Hill. Tradition has it that the front door of Milton Cottage is in Elsecar and the back door in Hoyland. George Palmer was well known throughout the district and is seen here during the 1950s with some of his squeeze-boxes. For a time he worked at Earl Fitzwilliam's Elsecar Main Colliery. After the Second World War and until his retirement he worked as a crane driver at Arthur Lee's steelworks. Among the many activities which occupied his spare time, he ran a Sunday Music Club at Milton Cottage for many years. This was attended by Joe Sabin (Hoyland's jovial barber, from King Street), Pikie White and others. *(Kevin Cooper)*

William Thomas Spencer Wentworth-Fitzwilliam, 6th Earl Fitzwilliam KG, DCL, DL (1815–1902), second son of the 5th Earl and Mary, fourth daughter of Thomas 1st Lord Dundas and Lady Charlotte, his wife, second daughter of William, 3rd Earl Fitzwilliam. After his elder brother's death on 8 November 1835 he became heir to the earldom and took on his brother's courtesy title of Viscount Milton. As Viscount Milton, like his elder brother, he also served as an MP, first being elected for Malton in 1837. In 1841 he was elected for the West Riding and in 1846 was again elected for Malton. In 1847 and for a further ten years, until he succeeded to the earldom, he was MP for County Wicklow. This Earl was one of the wealthiest Englishmen during the nineteenth century and on his death in 1902, he was worth the equivalent (calculated in 2000) of £3.3 billion, making him the third wealthiest person to have lived in England during the twentieth century. He was also the first Earl Fitzwilliam to be liable to death duties, the iniquitous tax introduced by Gladstone. The 6th Earl and his wife Countess Harriet had eight sons and six daughters. The first name of all eight sons was William – Viscount Milton MP (1839–77), William Henry, William Thomas, William Charles, William John, William George, William Hugh and William Reginald. All the daughters included Mary as one of their names.

Lord Fitzwilliam was an enthusiastic huntsman. He was master of two packs of hounds, Earl Fitzwilliam's (Wentworth) Hounds and Earl Fitzwilliam's (Grove) Hounds. At one time the Earl was hunting three days a week with the Wentworth hounds, one with the Grove and one with the Badsworth. Then on a Friday evening he would travel to Liverpool from his private railway station at Elsecar in order to cross to Ireland, where on Saturday he would hunt on his Irish estate at Coollattin. *(Author's collection)*

The 6th Earl Fitzwilliam died on 20 February 1902. He was buried in a brick-lined grave next to his wife. Their double grave is seen here shortly after the Earl's funeral. *(Roy Young)*

Harriet, Countess Fitzwilliam (1818–95), wife of the 6th Earl. Lady Frances Harriet Douglas, eldest daughter of George Sholto, 17th Earl of Morton, was like her husband held in great affection by their tenants and workforce. It has been suggested that the Fitzwilliam brothers, the sons of the 6th Earl and Countess Harriet, were all hot-blooded philanderers. If local rumours are true, there are indeed many descendants of illegitimate Fitzwilliam offspring living locally. After all, it was the 6th Earl who was responsible for opening the Fitzwilliam Orphanage in Cortworth Lane, as a home for boys taken into the Fitzwilliam Guardianship. Eight hot-blooded Fitzwilliam gentlemen let loose among the young female population could soon fill an orphanage, and by all accounts their father was not averse to the odd spot of extra-marital dalliance. When their youngest son, Reginald, succeeded in getting one of the maids pregnant, Countess Harriet was heard to remark 'Thank God, I was beginning to think he wasn't entire.' Perhaps the final part of the inscription on the plaque which adorns the front of the former orphanage, a complex of buildings now usually referred to as the Cortworth Boxes, which states 'This Boys Home was transferred to the Gordons Boys Home in 1900', is an indicator that the Fitzwilliam 'foundlings' had finally come of age and there was no longer a need to house them locally at the expense of the Earl. *(Author's collection)*

William, Viscount Milton (1839–77). Other than what he wrote himself, not a great deal had been recorded about the life of this particular member of the Fitzwilliam family until quite recently. More information has come to light about this most unusual Fitzwilliam, who despite being heir to the earldom seems to have been something of an outcast. Secrecy surrounds much of his life, but Michael Shaw Bond, a great-great-grandson of Lord Milton, descended through Milton's youngest daughter, Theresa, has, through some detective work, uncovered some fascinating information. It transpires that Lord Milton and his Cambridge friend, personal physician and travelling companion, Dr Cheadle, set out to travel across what is now western Canada. The story of this expedition was told in their book *The North-West Passage by Land*, published in 1865. The book was a huge success but Lord Milton's exploits were not generally favoured by the family, who appeared to regard this heir to the earldom as not a very Fitzwilliamesque Fitzwilliam. William, Viscount Milton, died in Rouen, France, on Wednesday 17 January 1877, aged thirty-seven. He was brought home to Wentworth and buried in the Fitzwilliam vault in the Old Church. Michael Shaw Bond set out to trace the journey undertaken by his ancestor and his companion. The account of his journey was published in Canada in 2001. *Way out West*, subtitled *On the Trail of an Errant Ancestor*, makes interesting reading. It highlights some of the taboos and well-kept secrets that exist even in the best of families. *(Michael Shaw Bond)*

Laura, Viscountess Milton (1849–86). William, Viscount Milton, married Laura Beauclerk, second daughter of the late Lord Charles Beauclerk, fourth son of William, 8th Duke of St Albans, at St George's Church, Hanover Square, London, on 10 August 1867. Lord Charles Beauclerk had been killed in 1861 trying to rescue the crew of a lifeboat off Scarborough. The Miltons' eldest child, a daughter, was born in 1869 and named Laura; then came Mabel (later Lady Mabel Smith, after whom Lady Mabel College was named). William (known as Billy) was born in Canada on 25 July 1872 and brought to Wentworth, where he was baptised that November. He was given the name De Meuron, because he was born at Pointe de Meuron, where his parents rented an isolated farmhouse at a bend on the Kaministiquia River north of Lake Superior. The Miltons' youngest child, Theresa, followed soon after. Laura, Viscountess Milton, died while on holiday in Torquay on 20 March 1886. Her body arrived at Wentworth in a lead shell encased within an elm coffin. Before her burial in a compartment next to her husband in the Fitzwilliam vault, in the Old Church, Lady Milton's lead and elm coffins were placed in yet another specially made oak coffin. *(Michael Shaw Bond)*

William Charles De Meuron Wentworth-Fitzwilliam, 7th Earl Fitzwilliam KCVO, CBE, DSO, JP, DL (1872–1943). Billy, the 7th Earl, succeeded his grandfather to the earldom in 1902. He was born in Canada and educated at Eton and Trinity College, Cambridge. As Viscount Milton his military career began in 1892, when he was sent as an aide to the Marquess of Lansdowne. He subsequently went on to serve in the Oxford Light Infantry, and in 1900, while serving in South Africa, was promoted to Major, and awarded the Distinguished Service Order. He was elected MP for Wakefield in 1895. When the Territorial Army was formed in 1908 Lord Fitzwilliam raised the Wentworth Battery of the Royal Artillery. He was Lord Mayor of Sheffield in 1909. In 1896 he married the society beauty Lady Maud Dundas, daughter of the 1st Marquess of Zetland. They had five children, four girls and one boy: Lady Elfrida (afterwards Countess of Wharncliffe), Lady Joan, Lady Donatia, Lady Helena and William Henry Lawrence Peter, Viscount Milton (known as Peter). The 7th Earl was interested in engineering and this interest resulted in the production of the Simplex motor car and the Nearacar. This image, taken in Wentworth Park, shows the 7th Earl in his major's uniform, with one of the guns of the Wentworth Battery of the Royal Artillery. *(Roy Young)*

This is the very last Simplex to be made – in 1925 for the 7th Earl Fitzwilliam's personal use. The Simplex was more expensive than a Rolls-Royce. This one is now in the collection of Kelham Island Museum, Sheffield. *(Reproduced by courtesy of the Fitzwilliam (Wentworth) Estates)*

Maud, Countess Fitzwilliam OBE (1877–1967). She is seen here with her son Lord Milton, during a cruise taken as part of his coming of age celebrations. Countess Maud was a keen and highly skilled horsewoman and an accomplished amateur artist. An enthusiastic gardener, she was responsible for the rose gardens and Japanese garden at Wentworth Woodhouse, which are now incorporated in Wentworth Garden Centre. Neglected after the Second World War, when open-cast mining destroyed many garden features, Lady Maud's splendid gardens have been beautifully restored under the watchful eye of Tony Airey. *(Author's collection)*

As was customary in the Fitzwilliam family, shortly after her marriage to Viscount Milton in 1896 the former Lady Maud Dundas was asked to choose an oak tree on the family's estate at Wentworth to cut down for its timber. The tree was duly felled and the wood was then prepared and stored in the Estate Building Yard until it was required to build her coffin. In fact the wood was not required for another seventy years. The finished coffin is seen below in the Estate Bulding Yard in March 1967, shortly before it was taken to the Fitzwilliams' Malton Estate to collect the body of Maud, Dowager Countess Fitzwilliam. Left to right: Melvyn Butcher (painter), John Booth (clerk of works) Stanley Walker (blacksmith) and George Butcher (master carpenter and brother of Melvyn the painter). *(Roy Young)*

William Henry Lawrence Peter Wentworth Fitzwilliam, 8th Earl Fitzwilliam DSC (1910–48). Viscount Milton, the future 8th Earl and, following the births of his four sisters, the long-awaited son and heir of 'Billy' and his adored wife Maud, was born at his parents' town house at 4 Grosvenor Square, London, on 31 December 1910. The christening took place in the private chapel at Wentworth Woodhouse on Saturday 11 February 1911, conducted by the Revd R. Verini. Celebrations to mark the event took on gargantuan proportions; similar celebrations marked Lord Milton's coming of age. Two years after he came of age Lord Milton married Miss Olive Plunkett, daughter of the Bishop of Meath. The ceremony took place in St Patrick's Cathedral, Dublin (see pages 108 and 109). Their only child, a daughter, Lady Juliet, was born in 1935. Both as Lord Milton and later as Earl, Peter was tremendously popular. He was a keen sportsman and distinguished himself during the Second World War. He became the 8th Earl on the death of his father on 15 February 1943. Sadly he died tragically young in a plane crash on 13 May 1948. With no son and heir to follow him as Earl, and no brothers, it was necessary to go back to Peter's great-grandfather's offspring to find an heir. It was Eric Spencer Wentworth-Fitzwilliam, a son of the 6th Earl's fourth son, Sir William Charles Wentworth Fitzwilliam (1848–1925), who succeeded Peter as the 9th Earl. (M. Joan Burgin)

In this 1945 family photograph are, left to right, Olive, Countess Fitzwilliam (1911–75), Lady Juliet Wentworth-Fitzwilliam and the 8th Earl Fitzwilliam. Lady Juliet was only child of the 8th Earl and Olive, Countess Fitzwilliam (born 24 January 1935). Lady Juliet gained an MA at St Hilda's College, Oxford. She married the 6th Marquess of Bristol in 1960, by whom she had a son, Lord Nicholas Hervey (1961–98). Lord and Lady Bristol divorced in 1972. Lady Juliet subsequently married Somerset de Chair (1911–95), poet, author, soldier and former MP, with whom she had a daughter, Helena. Under her mother's marriage settlement, following the death of the 10th Earl Fitzwilliam, Lady Juliet inherited substantial family treasures from Wentworth Woodhouse, now administered by the Trustees of the Rt Hon. Olive Countess Fitzwilliam Chattels Settlement. After Mr de Chair's death at the age of eighty-three, Lady Juliet de Chair married Dr Peter Tadgell in 1997. (Roy Young)

Mourners entering the Fitzwilliams' private burial ground at Wentworth for the burial of the 8th Earl Fitzwilliam, 1948. Among the mourners seen here are Olive, Countess Fitzwilliam, Lady Juliet Wentworth-Fitzwilliam and Maud, Dowager Countess Fitzwilliam. *(Roy Young)*

Stanley Webb looks after the bearers' bowler hats at the funeral of the 8th Earl Fitzwilliam at Holy Trinity Church, Wentworth, May 1948. *(Roy Young)*

Eric Spencer Wentworth-Fitzwilliam, 9th Earl Fitzwilliam (1883–1952), seen here at the funeral of the 8th Earl in May 1948. This convivial member of the Fitzwilliam family delighted in introducing himself to complete strangers by his nickname 'Bottle and Bottle Eric'. His marriage to Miss Jessica Rowlands in 1912 had ended in divorce in 1917 and there were no children. He did not marry again. The 9th Earl died on 3 April 1952. He was buried in the Fitzwilliam private burial ground, close to his grandfather, the 6th Earl, and adjacent to his parents – the Hon. Sir W. Charles Wentworth-Fitzwilliam, who died in 1925 and Constance Ann, Lady Wentworth Fitzwilliam, who died in 1941. *(Roy Young)*

The funeral of the 9th Earl Fitzwilliam, April 1952. The pallbearers visible in the photograph are, left to right, Messrs B. Amos, C. White and G. Broadhead. The village undertaker, Mr W.G. Tradewell, can be seen adjusting the wreath. *(Roy Young)*

William Thomas George Wentworth-Fitzwilliam, 10th Earl Fitzwilliam. This last Earl Fitzwilliam was affectionately known locally as 'Lord Tom'. He was the 5th Earl's great-grandson and had inherited the Fitzwilliams' ancestral estate surrounding Milton Hall, near Peterborough, from his father. The Milton estate had been split from the Yorkshire and Irish estates in the 5th Earl's will. With this last Earl all the Fitzwilliam estates were once again united. The 10th Earl died on the evening of Friday 21 September 1979 at Wentworth Woodhouse, following a stroke. He was seventy-five. On his death all the Fitzwilliam titles became extinct. Lord Fitzwilliam's coffin was placed in the private chapel at Wentworth Woodhouse, before being taken to the Milton estate for his funeral service and burial. Shortly before his death Lord Fitzwilliam had passed the village of Wentworth to a charitable trust, known as the Fitzwilliam Wentworth Amenity Trust. Lord Fitzwilliam also disposed of many properties elsewhere on his estate at Wentworth, and gave Keppel's Column to Rotherham Metropolitan Borough Council. *(Reproduced by courtesy of the Fitzwilliam (Wentworth) Estates)*

The coffin bearing the body of the 10th Earl Fitzwilliam leaves Peterborough Cathedral on Thursday 27 September 1979 after a service conducted by the Bishop of Peterborough, the Rt Revd Douglas Feaver. In contrast to the formality of the service at the cathedral, Lord Fitzwilliam was laid to rest later in the day after a simple ceremony in the quiet country churchyard of St Mary's Church, Marholm. *(Roy Young)*

The grave of the 10th Earl Fitzwilliam in the churchyard of St Mary's Church, Marholm. Marholm is situated on the Fitzwilliams' ancestral estate, which surrounds Milton Hall. The Fitzwilliam family has been in residence there since 1503. Lord Fitzwilliam's grave faces towards Milton Hall. *(Paul T. Langley Welch)*

Countess Joyce (1898–1995), wife of the 10th Earl. Born Joyce Elizabeth Mary Langdale at Houghton Hall, in the West Riding of Yorkshire, she married Captain Howard Edward Fitzalan Howard in 1922. He succeeded to his father's viscountcy in 1947 as the 2nd Viscount Fitzalan of Derwent, and they had two daughters. They divorced in 1955 and the following year Lady Fitzalan of Derwent married the 10th Earl Fitzwilliam. There were no heirs to either of her husbands' titles and on their deaths their titles became extinct. *(Author's collection)*

The grave of Joyce, Countess Fitzwilliam in the churchyard of St Mary's Church, Marholm. Lady Fitzwilliam is buried next to her husband. *(Paul T. Langley Welch)*

Tom Roland Hill (1907–81), Manager of the EFW flour mill, Wath Road, Elsecar, outside the mill on 8 June 1972. The mill was taken over by Allied Mills Limited in the autumn of 1962. Tom Hill's new contract of employment as mill manager commenced on 15 October 1962. The mill was sold to Elsecar Stone Ground Flour Mills Limited, a subsidiary of Allied Mills Ltd. The sale was completed on 10 December 1962, when the mill, its dwelling house and office, and the scout hall (with a seven-year covenant that the scouts could remain there), covering an area of 1800 square yards, were sold on the instructions of the 10th Earl Fitzwilliam for £1,000. What a bargain! When his contract of employment was reviewed on 10 October 1976, Tom Hill's basic salary was £1,312 per annum, to be paid monthly in arrears. He was given four weeks' paid holiday per annum plus all bank and public holidays. As well as being mill manager, Mr Hill was involved with the Scout Association for many years. He was also a senior warden in the West Riding County Council Civil Defence Warden Service. He was awarded the Civil Defence Long Service Medal in July 1962, and awarded the Medal of Merit, in recognition of his outstanding services to the scout movement, in 1968. On the day that he died in February 1981 Mr Hill was still working at the mill. He was taken ill while filling in the tax returns and taken to hospital, where he died later that day. His wife, Nelly, had died just a few weeks before on 17 December 1980. (*M. Joan Burgin*)

The Scout Association
South Yorkshire County

President: The Rt. Hon. THE EARL OF SCARBROUGH, K.G., P.C., G.C.S.I., G.C.I.E., G.C.V.O., H.M.L., T.D.

FROM MAJOR E. D. TURNER, THE COUNTY COMMISSIONER, TIMES OFFICE, MEXBOROUG[H]
Telephones Mexborough 2551 (Office) Maltby 2241 (Home).

29th March, 1968.

T. R. Hill, Esq.,
G.S.L. 11th Wentworth (Elsecar),
Mill House,
Wath Road,
Elsecar,
Nr. Barnsley.

Dear Mr. Hill,

I have much pleasure in informing you that the Chief Scout has awarded you the Medal of Merit in recognition of your outstanding services to the Movement. He has particularly asked me to convey to you his sincere congratulations and best wishes.

At the same time, I would also like to add my own personal congratulations and thanks for the dedicated service which you have given to Scouting throughout the years.

I shall look forward to presenting this award to you on the first suitable occasion. I will make the necessary arrangements with your Acting District Commissioner, who will no doubt be contacting you in due course.

Thank you very much again for all the hard work you have put in.

Yours sincerely,

County Commissioner.

A letter from Major E.D. Turner, the County Commissioner of the Scout Association. *(M. Joan Burgin)*

The Scout Association
South Yorkshire County

FROM MR. R. S. BRUCE, THE HON. COUNTY SECRETARY, BRUCE BROTHERS (SHEFFIELD) LTD.,
PELHAM WORKS, SYLVESTER GARDENS, SHEFFIELD 1.
Telephones Sheffield 29871 (Office)   Sheffield 363122 (Home).

RSB/JMB

29th April, 1968

T. R. Hill, Esq.,
Mill House,
Wath Road,
Elsecar,
Barnsley.

Dear Roland,

I was delighted to have the opportunity of presenting you with your Medal of Merit on Friday night and enclose herewith a copy of the citation for you to retain.

Yours sincerely,

A letter from Mr R.S. Bruce, Hon. County Secretary of the Scout Association. *(M. Joan Burgin)*

The Scout Association
South Yorkshire County

FROM MR. R. S. BRUCE, THE HON. COUNTY SECRETARY, BRUCE BROTHERS (SHEFFIELD) LTD., PELHAM WORKS, SYLVESTER GARDENS, SHEFFIELD 1.

Telephones Sheffield 29871 (Office)   Sheffield 363122 (Home).

Mr. Tom Roland Hill has been in Scouting for 50 years.   He joined the Wentworth troop in 1917 where he later became A.S.M. Leaving there to go to High Green in 1930 to start a Wolf Cub Section;   leaving High Green in 1935 and still keeping his interest.

In October 1953 he took charge of the 11th Wentworth (Elsecar) troop.   Through his driving force the group have their own headquarters.   This was originally an old barn which was stripped and reconstructed by Scouts and lay members under his guidance and supervision.   He gave up a great deal of time for this labour of love, helped by his wife, who was an active member of his group committee, also his son and daughter who hold Warrants with the same troop, where he himself is still active.

By his means, hundreds of boys have been given not only first class training, but moral benefit of a great example of leadership.   He is justly held in high esteem, not only in Scouting and by hundreds of Scouts and old Scouts, but by the people of Elsecar district, amongst whom for many years he has set such an excellent example of social service.

The citation for Tom Roland Hill's Medal of Merit. *(M. Joan Burgin)*

5
Holidays, Outings, Events, Sports & Pastimes

Mrs Martha Nelder of 81 Church Street, Elsecar, and
her nephew Geoffrey, aged three and a half, on
Humberstone beach, 1959. *(Martha Nelder)*

Birdwell Cricket Club, now the Rockingham Centre, early twentieth century. *(Keith Robinson collection)*

Elsecar Congregational Church Football Team 1917/18. *(Edwin Moody collection)*

This image, which dates from the late 1920s or early 1930s, shows Jim Doughty (1906–56) on the right, winner of Hoyland Miners' Welfare Bowling Tournament. Mr Thompson (runner-up) is beside him. Jim Doughty was brought up in Elizabeth Street, Rock Mount, Hoyland. Sadly the lovely crown green bowling green at the corner of Millhouses Street and King Street was abandoned in January 2002, after members grew tired of repeated break-ins at the clubhouse and vandalism to the grounds and to the green itself. Once again, because of selfish acts by less upstanding members of the local community, the area has lost another amenity. *(David Doughty collection)*

Elsecar Park, 1934. Two Hoyland boys enjoying the delights of Elsecar-by-the-Sea: Jim Bowley and Bill Bowley (doing the crab), sons of Jim Bowley snr and Lily Bowley (see page 18). *(Theresa Whittlestone)*

Silver Jubilee celebrations in Noble Street, Hoyland, 1935. Back row, left to right: Doreen Nelder, Kathleen Turner, Nancy Lee, Doreen Parkin and Dorothy Dean. Front row: Walter Beardshall, Margaret Nelder, John Brooks, Kathleen Smith and Margaret Kay. *(Doreen Howse collection)*

Blackpool, 1938. Left to right: Terry Fletcher, Roy Fletcher (of Croft Road, Hoyland, see page 14) and John Leach (of Hoyland), a family friend. *(Theresa Whittlestone)*

The Moody family of 84 Strafford Avenue, Elsecar, on their summer holidays at Cleethorpes during August and early September 1939. While on holiday, on 3 September, war was declared. The Moodys stayed at 112 Poplar Road with a butcher called Baker, who ran a bed and breakfast establishment. The Bakers' son, Cyril, was in the RAF and lost his life during the conflict. Seen here are Clara and Horace Moody with their sons Kenneth (right) and Edwin. After the Second World War, Mr and Mrs Baker and their daughter, Joyce, visited the Moody family at their home in Elsecar. Joyce came to stay with the Moodys for several years afterwards. *(Edwin Moody collection)*

Harrison (Sony) Bailey (born 19 November 1916), Monsal Dale, summer 1940. Sony was a keen and accomplished cyclist. At the time of this photograph Sony was working at Cortonwood Colliery. He later worked at Hall and Pickles in Chapeltown, where he remained until his retirement. He had joined Barnsley Road Club in 1936 and remained a member until 1942, when he joined Sheffield Phoenix Cycling Club. In 1945 he resigned his membership and once again joined the Barnsley Road Club, and remained a member until an industrial injury to his knee compelled him to give up competitive cycling in 1965. He took up fell walking instead, at which he became equally accomplished. *(Kevin Cooper)*

Barnsley Road Club members, Monsal Dale, summer 1940. The Monsal Head public house can be seen in the background. Left to right: Jack Simpson (of Excelsior Terrace, Birdwell), Ernest Nixon (from Tankersley), Sony Bailey (of King Street, Hoyland) and Jim Carr (of Hay Green Lane, Birdwell). Club members used to meet at Town End, Barnsley. *(Harrison Bailey)*

A small singing group known as Hoyland's Bright Sunbeams, 1951. Back row, left to right: Betty Locket, Janet Peasgood, Susan Taylor, Brenda Taylor. Front row: Janet Locket and Terry Gallagher. The photo was taken in the Lockets' yard in Hunt Street, Hoyland Common. *(Terry Gallagher)*

The Ladies Friendship Circle at Elsecar Congregational Church, late 1950s. Left to right: Frances Hargreaves, Doris Clarke, Mary Hague, May Armitage, Mary Fenton, Margaret Hewitt. Daisy Noble, Mary Walton, Bessie Oliver, Margaret Holliday, Margaret Dodson and Clara Massingham. *(Mary Fenton)*

Jimmy Barraclough's dancing class at their
medal presentation at the Miners' Welfare Hall,
King Street, Hoyland, late 1950s. Mr
Barraclough held his dancing classes (Old
Time) in a hall behind 63 and 65 St Helen's
Street. These houses were once a public house
known as the Wharncliffe Arms. Among those
pictured are Trevor Thrush, Peter Shaw, Denise
Whitworth, Pauline Bell, Geraldine Sleath,
Christine Howse, Kathleen Marples, Carol
Slater, Irene Jepson, Sharon Scothorn, Denise
Scothorn, Rita Widdowson, Jennifer Papworth
and Maureen Thrush. The boy in the white
tuxedo (front right) is Tony Scothorn, who was
later to find fame as Sheffield Wednesday's
goal-keeper. *(Christine Walker)*

Miss Christine Howse (now Mrs Walker) of
8 Ebenezer Place and Master Roger Barton
from Hoyland Common, accomplished Old
Time Dancing juniors, pupils of Jimmy
Barraclough. *(Herbert and Doreen Howse)*

Gilbert and Anne Cooper on holiday in Ireland, 1959 (see pages 116–18). Mrs Cooper was noted for wearing hats and carrying a matching handbag. During the holiday the Coopers went boating on the lake, seen here. While attempting to get into a comfortable position Mrs Cooper fell out of the boat and into the water. Fortunately the boat was near the bank and the water reasonably shallow. Her husband was relieved to see his wife unharmed and delighted that, despite her tumble, she was still wearing her characteristic hat and clutching her handbag. *(Theresa Whittlestone)*

This fancy dress party took place at the Strafford Arms on Saturday 20 March 1971. Left to right: Roy Allen, Jack Parkin, Margaret Allen (as Mary Queen of Scots), Frank Andrews, Betty Andrews, Derek Porter, Shirley Moxon and, in the guise of King Henry VIII, George Arthur Hopson (landlord). *(Joan Hopson)*

A group of fifth- and sixth-formers from Kirk Balk School during their ten-day, 240-mile sponsored walk of the Pennine Way, Easter holidays, 1973. The walk started at Hadrians Wall and finished at Edale. Shortly after their arrival at the starting point, just before they were about to leave the old air force bus which had taken them from Hoyland, it was announced on the radio that two of the greatest figures of the twentieth century had died, Sir Noël Coward and Pablo Picasso. In the photograph are, left to right, Kevin Cooper, Brian Oxley, Gillian Oxley (Brian's twin), Stephen Cooke, Derek Rodgers, David Burrows and Geoffrey Howse. *(Author's collection)*

The party from Kirk Balk School on their journey along the Pennine Way. They spent the night at the youth hostel, seen in the background, at Hawes. Pictured are Stephen Cooke, Derek Rodgers, Brenda Clough, David Burrows (wearing hat), Geoffrey Howse, Kevin Cooper, Gillian Oxley and Brian Oxley. *(Author's collection)*

Hoyland Springwood Junior and Infants School, fancy dress parade, 1978. Among those featured are Alison Hoyland, Louise Hague, Maxine Bagnall, Rachael Wadsworth, Gary Watson, Caroline Camm and Theresa Fletcher. (*Theresa Whittlestone*)

Theresa Fletcher (now Mrs Whittlestone), 'Queen of Hearts', aged eight, winner of the Hoyland Springwood Junior and Infants School fancy dress parade, in 1978. (*Theresa Whittlestone*)

The Ireland Alloys Band, named in 1977 when Ireland Alloys began to sponsor the band formerly known as the Hoyland Town Silver Prize Band, seen here in 1979. Among those pictured are: R. Leake, N. Buckle, A. Knight, R. Williams, R. Riggett, T. Milner, K. Lockwood, C. Cautley, J. Francis, R. Nixon, P. Wilkinson, B. Lyons, V. Wordsworth, P. Proost, E. Hambling, P. Ward, D. Cautley, P. Foreman, J. Wadsworth, C. Williams, C. Lord, C. Davis, P. Lewis, S. Davis and M. Grimes. *(Joan Hopson)*

The Walker family of South View Road, Hoyland, on holiday at Lands End, June 1980. Back row, left to right: Darren Walker, Ivan Walker and Adam Walker. Front row: David Walker, Suki Walker and Christine Walker. *(Doreen Howse collection)*

This early 1980s view shows the popular local majorettes, the Hoylandaires, in Armroyd Lane, marching to Elsecar Park. In the background can be seen some of the cottages in Fitzwilliam Street built by the Fitzwilliam family in the nineteenth century. The gap in the buildings near the double-decker bus – the Elsecar Circular – shows where cottages have been demolished. Work is still taking place at Fitzwilliam Lodge (the Bun and Milk Club), which reopened, after being converted into fourteen flats, in 1982. *(Mary Fenton)*

The 18th Barnsley Scouts (from Hoyland), called the 13th Wentworth until 1974, after which they took on a new name to reflect Hoyland's association with the new Metropolitan Borough of Barnsley. Here they are marching along Market Street, Hoyland, towards the Scout Hall. They are just passing Tithe Lane and the top of Barber Street. Leading the troupe is Barry Lipscombe. The standard bearer is Darren Walker and front right (wearing spectacles) is Andrew Owen. *(David and Christine Walker)*

Three Hoyland ladies enjoying the fancy dress evening at the Royal York Hotel, Ryde, Isle of Wight, early 1990s. This was a regular and popular short break for a large group from Hoyland over several years. Dressed as St Trinian's girls are, left to right, Mrs Margaret Booth, Mrs Doreen Howse and Mrs Sylvia Steel. *(Doreen Howse collection)*

6
Weddings

Doreen Nelder, 22 June 1946, shortly before she was joined
in holy matrimony to Herbert Howse at Holy Trinity
Church, Elsecar. *(Herbert and Doreen Howse)*

John Henry Tollerfield, aged twenty-one, and his wife Sarah, aged twenty-four, seen here in 1900, following their wedding at St Peter's Church, Hoyland. *(David Doughty collection)*

An Edwardian wedding. pictured outside 178 Wath Road, Elsecar (Rhubarb Row). Back row, left to right: Mr Greenfield, Mrs Greenfield (née Marion Knock), the Revd J. Makinson, Mrs Knock (mother), Arthur Waters, Mrs Waters (née Sarah Ann Nock), Mr Nock (father), Mrs J. Firth, Mr W. Firth and Mrs W. Firth. Middle row: Mrs Walker (grandmother) Mrs Nock (grandmother) and Miss Schofield (friend). Front row: Miss Firth, Mrs Senior, -?-, Mrs Hill, Lillian Nock, Annis Nock, Mrs J. Walker and Mr A. Walker. *(Keith Robinson collection)*

The wedding of Clara Evans and Horace Moody at Holy Trinity Church, Elsecar, 10 June 1919. The the Revd Charles Molesworth Sharpe (pictured on page 106) conducted the ceremony. Horace Moody (1892–1978) and Clara, his wife (1896–1985), first lived after their marriage in a house belonging to Moses Bailey in Dick Croft, Hoyland (later known as High Croft). During the General Strike in 1926 the Moodys moved to 84 Strafford Avenue, Elsecar, where they resided until their deaths. *(Edwin Moody collection)*

The Revd Charles Charles Molesworth Sharpe MA was inducted as vicar of Elsecar on 11 December 1888, having previously been curate at St Peter's Church, Tankersley, to the Revd Alexander Macnaughton (both were Earl Fitzwilliam's livings). He was a popular and outspoken vicar, who after his retirement in November 1922 was much missed by his parishioners. *(Keith Robinson collection)*

Horace and Clara Moody at their golden wedding anniversary party, held in the School Room at Elsecar Congregational Church, Hill Street, 10 June 1969. Also pictured are their younger son Kenneth and his daughter Cathryn. *(Edwin Moody collection)*

Guests at the golden wedding anniversary party of Horace and Clara Moody in the grounds of Elsecar Congregational Church, 10 June 1969. Back row, left to right: Frank Evans, Kenneth Webb, Eileen Webb, Kenneth Moody, Arthur Sherlock, Roland Fenton, Ruth Evans, Doreen Fenton and Teresa Stamp. Front row: Mrs Eric Evans, Cathryn Moody, Mrs Sarah Sherlock, Mrs Clara Moody, Mr Horace Moody, Mr and Mrs Walter Evans. *(Edwin Moody collection)*

The wedding of Anne Bowley to Roy Fletcher at St Andrew's Church, Hoyland, 14 May 1932. The Revd Crowther Alwyn conducted the service. *(Theresa Whittlestone)*

The garden of 60 Longfields Crescent, Hoyland, following the wedding of Anne Bowley and Roy Fletcher, 14 May 1932. Back row, left to right: Annie Jessop, Jim Bowley jnr, Bill Bowley, Mr Hoole, -?-, Nellie Hatton. Front row: -?-, Ethel Oliver, Roy Fletcher, Anne Fletcher (née Bowley), -?- and Viv Dickinson. *(Theresa Whittlestone)*

The wedding of William Henry Lawrence Peter Wentworth-Fitzwilliam, Viscount Milton, to Miss Olive Plunkett, daughter of the late Hon. and Most Revd Dr Benjamin J. Plunkett, Bishop of Meath, 19 April 1933, in St Patrick's Cathedral, Dublin. Over a hundred estate employees travelled to Ireland at the expense of the 7th Earl Fitzwilliam to attend the wedding of his only son and heir. *(Roy Young)*

The wedding of Dorothy Whorton to James Arthur Hague, at St John's Chapel, Elsecar, 3 August 1936. The presiding minister was Peter Hutchinson. The bride's father was well-known Hoyland butcher Leonard Whorton, who ran his business from lock-up premises on Market Street, opposite the grounds of Hoyland Hall. *(Christine Short)*

The wedding of Blanche Senior to Gerald
Stainrod at Parkgate, Rotherham, 1938.
Walter Senior, of Spring Gardens, Hoyland
(see page 16) took over an off-licence in
Parkgate on his retirement. The bridesmaid
seated extreme right is Bessie Barlow; her
husband stands behind her. The pageboy next
to Bessie is Gerald Cowood (son of Blanche,
née Senior) and Mary Senior is next to him.
Standing next to Mr Barlow (back right) is
Percy Senior and next to him his father,
William. The pageboy on the left is Douglas
Hutton. *(Mary Fenton)*

Douglas Hutton and Gerald Cowood, pageboys
at the wedding of Blanche Senior and Gerald
Stainrod, in 1938. *(Mary Fenton)*

The wedding of Martha Howse of 3 Wentworth Road, Elsecar to George Nelder of Foundry Street, at Holy Trinity Church, Elsecar, 22 July 1939. After a honeymoon in Oxfordshire, the newlyweds moved into their new home at 81 Church Street, Elsecar. *(Herbert and Doreen Howse)*

The wedding cake of Martha Howse and George Nelder, decorated by Nellie Lambert (née Bamforth). *(Martha Nelder)*

The wedding of Avice Hague to Geoffrey Walker on 1 January 1940, at St Andrew's Church, Hoyland. Among those present are Mr and Mrs I.L. Walker (parents of Geoffrey, from Hoyland's well-known newsagents), Miss Joan Walker, Tommy and Audrey Thurgoland, Mr Arthur and Mrs Dorothy Hague and Miss Christine Hague. The little girl was Miss Audrey Rothwell, a relation of the Walkers and an evacuee from London. *(David and Christine Walker)*

The wedding of Emmie Fannon of Hoyland to Wilfred Cooper, 7 May 1940. The marriage ceremony took place at Barnsley Register Office. *(Emmie Cooper)*

The wedding of Doreen Nelder (see page 12) to Herbert Howse of Church Street, Elsecar, 22 June 1946. Left to right: Joan Howse, Joseph Royston, Florence Jubb, Herbert Howse, Doreen Howse, George Nelder, Terence Nelder, Stanley Nelder, Margaret Nelder. The service took place at Holy Trinity Church, Elsecar. The bride was given away by her brother George Nelder, and the Revd Walter H. de Voil officiated. *(Herbert and Doreen Howse)*

The Revd Walter H. de Voil LTh (Dunelm), MA, PhD (Edinburgh), Vicar of Elsecar. Dr de Voil was inducted as vicar of Elsecar on 23 July 1942. He took his last service as vicar of that parish on 23 January 1949. *(M. Joan Burgin)*

The wedding of Kathleen Airey of Street Cottages, Wentworth, to John (Jack) Howse, second son of Mr and Mrs Isadore Howse of Elsecar, at Holy Trinity Church, Wentworth, 26 March 1952. Left to right: Joan Howse, Terence Nelder, Clara Susannah Howse and her husband Isadore Howse, John Howse, Kathleen Howse, Oscar and Edith Airey, Herbert Howse, Jean Fuller and Tony Fuller. The reception took place in the Fitzwilliam Room at the Rockingham Arms, where fifty years later Jack and Kathy Howse celebrated their golden wedding anniversary. *(Herbert and Doreen Howse)*

The wedding of Eleanor Woodhead of Brampton and Stanley Nelder of Elsecar (see page 12) at Cortonwood Chapel, Brampton, 23 August 1952. In August 2002, the couple celebrated their golden wedding at Leven, where they own a holiday home. *(Doreen Howse collection)*

The wedding of Anne Fletcher (née Bowley, widow of Roy Fletcher, see pages 14 and 107) to Gilbert Cooper, 1953. Mrs Fletcher is seen here on her arrival at St Andrew's Church, Hoyland, with her brother Jim Bowley jnr who gave her away. *(Theresa Whittlestone)*

Mr and Mrs Gilbert Cooper pause for the photographer before entering the limousine that will take them to their wedding reception at St Andrew's School Room, Market Street, Hoyland. *(Theresa Whittlestone)*

Mr and Mrs Gilbert Cooper at their wedding reception at St Andrew's School Room. Anne made and decorated her own wedding cake. She was well known locally for her cake decoration, which she continued until old age. She was also a serving sister with the St John Ambulance Brigade. *(Theresa Whittlestone)*

Another photograph taken at Gilbert and Anne Cooper's wedding reception. Left to right: Gilbert Cooper, Jim Bowley snr, the Revd Geoffrey Surtees (vicar of St Andrew's 1939–57), Lily Bowley and Anne Cooper. The newlyweds spent their honeymoon in Jersey and Guernsey. *(Theresa Whittlestone)*

The wedding of Marlene Linley and Keith Bamforth at St Andrew's Church, Hoyland, 1957. *(Doreen Howse collection)*

The wedding of Margaret Barrow of Vizard Road, Elsecar, to Albert Leathers of Birdwell at Holy Trinity Church, Elsecar, August 1957. *(Doreen Howse collection)*

This wedding took place at Hoyland's former parish church, All Saints Church, Wath-upon-Dearne, December 1959. Kathleen (née Foers) of Wath-upon-Dearne and Robert A. Dale of Platts Common are seen here shortly after the marriage ceremony. *(Robert and Kathleen Dale)*

The wedding of Barbara Jones of 17 Main Street, Wentworth, to Terence Nelder of 81 Church Street, Elsecar. The ceremony took place at Holy Trinity Church, Wentworth (the New Church) on 30 March 1964. Left to right: Martha Nelder, George Nelder (see pages 91 and 112), groom and bride, Harry Jones and Mrs Dorothy Jones. *(Herbert and Doreen Howse)*

The wedding of Margaret Nelder of Thorpe Hesley (see page 12) and Clifford Willoughby of Thorpe Hesley at St John's Church, Chapeltown, 16 July 1966. Left to right: Walter Willoughby, Lily Willoughby, Clifford Willoughby, Margaret Willoughby, Christine Howse and Stephen Willoughby. *(Clifford Willoughby and Margaret Willoughby)*

The wedding of Margaret Nelder to Clifford Willoughby (see previous page). Left to right: George H. Nelder, Mrs M. Nelder (see page 112), Herbert Howse, Doreen Howse (see page 114), Clifford Willoughby, Margaret Willoughby, Christine Howse, Eleanor Nelder and Stanley Nelder (see page 115). *(Clifford Willoughby and Margaret Willoughby)*

The newly married couple, Clifford and Margaret Willoughby, about to leave for their honeymoon in Torquay in their Riley 1.5. *(Clifford Willoughby and Margaret Willoughby)*

The wedding of Christine Howse of Manor Way, Hoyland, to David Walker of West Street, Hoyland, at St Peter's Church, Hoyland, 1 January 1968. The wedding ceremony was conducted by the Revd Wilfred Clark. During the ceremony well-known soprano Ruth Wainwright sang 'Ave Maria'. The marriage ceremony was followed by a reception at the Queen's Hotel, Barnsley. *(Herbert and Doreen Howse)*

The wedding of Pamela Howse of Street Cottages, Wentworth, to David Greenfield of Booth Street, Hoyland, 3 January 1973. Darren Walker presents a lucky chimney sweep to the bride, while her husband looks on. *(Herbert and Doreen Howse)*

The marriage of Lyn Dale of Manor Way, Hoyland, to Ronald Melling at St Andrew's Church, Hoyland, 15 August 1981. Left to right: groom, bride, Steven Holdsworth (best man), Lesley Ayres, Karen Hoyle, Mandy Hoyle, Jane Melling, Rachael Fisher. The bride's brother, Steven Dale, is on the right. *(Robert and Kathleen Dale)*

Mark and Theresa Whittlestone are seen here at their wedding reception, which took place at the Queen's Hotel, Barnsley. *(Theresa Whittlestone)*

The marriage of Theresa Fletcher to
Mark Whittlestone took place at
St Peter's Church, Hoyland, on 21 July
1990. The bride and groom were both
aged twenty. They are seen here with
Mark's brother and best man, Richard,
aged seventeen. *(Theresa Whittlestone)*

The wedding of Jenny McDermott of
Manor Way, Hoyland, to Craig Jacobs
at St Andrew's Church, Hoyland,
Saturday 3 August 2002. *(Mr and Mrs
C. Jacobs)*

ACKNOWLEDGEMENTS

Iwould like to thank my personal assistant John D. Murray, Harrison Bailey, Michael Shaw Bond, Tony Briggs of Harvey and Richardson, Hoyland, M. Joan Burgin, Guy R. Canby FRICS, Agent to the Fitzwilliam (Wentworth) Estates, Arthur K. Clayton BEM, Emmie Cooper, Kevin Cooper, Robert and Kathleen Dale, Tracy P. Deller, Ricky S. Deller, Joanna C. Murray Deller, David Doughty, Mary Fenton, George and Wendy Floyd, Terry Gallagher, Joan Hopson, Herbert and Doreen Howse, John (Jack) and Kathleen Howse, Mr and Mrs C. Jacobs, Ethel Jones (Estate Office, Wentworth), Brenda Loy, Peter Marsh, Edwin Moody, Robert Henry Mower, Martha Nelder, Jack Oliver, Sheila Margaret Ottley, Keith and Mavis Robinson, Chris Sharp of Old Barnsley, Harold Short, Christine Short, Cyril Slinn, Edwin Hugh Stenton and Amy Stenton, Lindy Stevenson, Estate Surveyor, Fitzwilliam (Wentworth) Estates, Ian J. Stewart, David and Christine Walker of Walkers Newsagents, Hoyland, Ralph Walker, Rex Walker, Mark and Theresa Whittlestone, Clifford and Margaret Willoughby, Roy Young. My thanks also go to Simon Fletcher, Anne Bennett, Glad Stockdale, Jeremy Yates-Round and Michelle Tilling of Sutton Publishing.

Paul T. Langley Welch, who has taken some of the more recent photographs featured in this book, works as a freelance theatrical and commercial photographer. He has worked with Geoffrey Howse on several projects since the 1980s and has taken photographs for several of Geoffrey's books.

The author and Lindy Stevenson, Surveyor, Fitzwilliam (Wentworth) Estates, near the Great South Terrace at Wentworth, above Bessie Gill's Spring, during an extensive photographic study of the estate conducted by the author and Paul T. Langley Welch. *(Reproduced by courtesy of the Fitzwilliam (Wentworth) Estates)*